Mathematical development

Planning and Assessment **Stepping Stones** **Early Learning Goals** **Practical activity ideas**

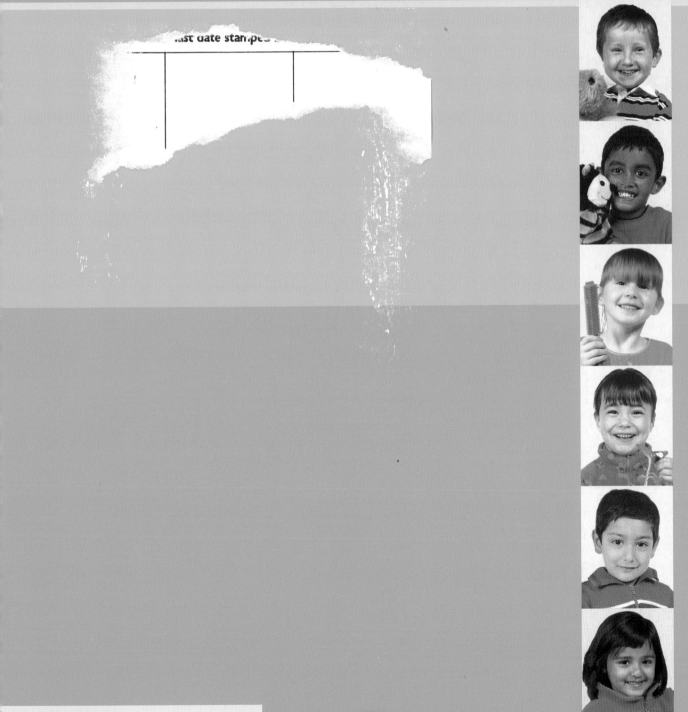

Jenni Tavener

Goals for the Foundation Stage

British Library Cataloguing-in-Publication Data A catalogue record for this book is available from the British Library.

ISBN 0 439 98351 7

The right of Jenni Tavener to be identified as the author of this work has been asserted by her in accordance with the Copyright, Designs and Patents Act 1988.

Author
Jenni Tavener

Editor
Saveria Mezzana

Designer
Heather C Sanneh

Assistant Editor
Victoria Lee

Illustrations
Rebecca Archer

Series Designer
Clare Brewer

Cover photography
Derek Cooknell

Text © 2003 Jenni Tavener
© 2003 Scholastic Ltd

For Gus Goodman

Designed using Adobe Pagemaker

Published by Scholastic Ltd,
Villiers House,
Clarendon Avenue,
Leamington Spa,
Warwickshire CV32 5PR

Visit our website at www.scholastic.co.uk
Printed by Proost NV, Belgium

2 3 4 5 6 7 8 9 0   5 6 7 8 9 0 1 2

Acknowledgements
Qualifications and Curriculum Authority for the use of extracts from the QCA/DfEE document *Curriculum Guidance for the Foundation Stage* © 2000 Qualifications and Curriculum Authority.
Every effort has been made to trace copyright holders and the publishers apologise for any inadvertent omissions.

Mathematical development

Contents

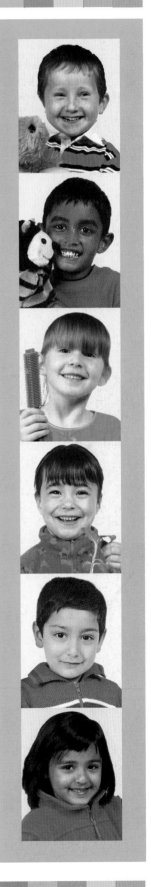

Goals for the Foundation Stage

Chapter 3   Shape, space and measures

Photocopiable pages

Mathematical development

Introduction

The *Goals for the Foundation Stage* series aims to provide educators and carers of children aged three to five with a range of practical activities to support the Early Learning Goals outlined in the document *Curriculum Guidance for the Foundation Stage* (QCA). Each book in this series focuses on one of the Areas of Learning. This book focuses on Mathematical development and is organised to provide a chapter for each cluster of Early Learning Goals. The activities suggested can be applied equally well to the documents on pre-school education published for Scotland, Wales and Northern Ireland.

The three clusters

Numbers as labels and for counting

The activities in this chapter aim to encourage the children to notice where numbers are used in their everyday environment, to help them to recognise number formation and to learn the number names. The activities also aim to involve the children in counting tasks such as saying the number names in order, matching numbers to objects, and finding out that, when counting, the last number that they say gives them the total number of objects in a group.

Calculating

This chapter gives you ideas to help the children to use numbers in a variety of practical contexts. They will be involved in talking about numbers, making deductions and comparing numbers. This chapter also offers ideas to introduce the children to combining numbers in simple addition and subtraction activities.

Shape, space and measures

With the activities in this chapter, the children will gain an awareness of two-dimensional and three-dimensional objects and shapes. They will be challenged to recognise similarities and differences in shapes, and to explore the properties of shapes. For example, they will learn how to distinguish flat shapes from solid shapes, how to recognise shapes in the environment, and they will find out which shapes roll and which do not. Ideas are also provided to encourage an awareness of space by involving the children in building models, creating patchwork patterns and following positional or directional clues.

Structure of the book

The first two chapters in the book focus on planning and assessment for Mathematical development. The chapter on planning will help you to plan your activities for the short, medium and long term, and the chapter on assessment explains the importance of assessing the children in your setting and gives you ideas and advice on how to achieve this.

Mathematical development

Introduction

The next three chapters offer a range of ideas that link directly to the Early Learning Goals within each cluster. The activities also support the appropriate Stepping Stones.

A section at the end of the book provides a range of photocopiable resources such as assessment sheets, activity sheets and number games.

The activities within this book provide a scope of ideas to involve the children in a variety of experiences that encourage and develop mathematical skills as they progress through the Foundation Stage. Ideas include making a footprint number track based on a popular rhyme, constructing humorous 'Block-bugs' for a floor game, decorating 'fish' for an interactive display, finding and counting pretend jewels hidden in a sand tray and programming a toy to move.

Many of the activities can also be used to help the children to develop communication and social skills such as listening to instructions, co-operating during a number game, sharing resources and working as a team.

How to use this book

Each activity chapter includes 20 activities that follow the same format, with the following sections: 'Stepping Stone', colour-coded to show whether the activity is at the simplest level (yellow), at a higher level (blue) or at the highest level (green) to match the colours used to show progression in the document *Curriculum Guidance for the Foundation Stage*; 'Early Learning Goal'; 'Group size'; 'What you need'; 'Preparation' (where appropriate); 'What to do', with the last two bullet-pointed ideas offering ways to simplify the idea for younger or less able children, and

to extend the idea for older or more able children; 'More ideas', which provides further mathematical ideas to achieve the same Stepping Stone or Early Learning Goal; 'Other curriculum areas', which gives further ideas to achieve the same Early Learning Goal through other Areas of Learning, identified in the shortened form of PSED (Personal, social and emotional development), CLL (Communication, language and literacy), MD (Mathematical development), KUW (Knowledge and understanding of the world), PD (Physical development) and CD (Creative development); and finally, 'Home links', which suggests ways that parents and carers can be involved in helping their children to achieve the Early Learning Goal.

How to use the photocopiable sheets

There are 18 photocopiable sheets in this book, which can be found on pages 79–96, all aiming to back up or extend the activity ideas. The first three photocopiable sheets are assessment sheets (one for each cluster of Early Learning Goals, and each chapter in this book) and can be used to keep an ongoing record of each child's attainment, throughout the Foundation Stage, as they progress through the Early Learning Goals.

The other photocopiable sheets use a variety of approaches to help to stimulate the children's interest in mathematical themes, for example, creating number cards, decorating number mobiles and completing puzzles. Most of these sheets can also be used as 'stand-alone' activity sheets, to help to develop or reinforce number skills such as number recognition, counting back and matching shapes.

Links with other curriculum areas

Many of the activities in this book can be linked to other areas of the curriculum. Personal, social and emotional development can be encouraged through number game activities by providing opportunities for the children to co-operate, take turns and play fairly with one another.

Communication, language and literacy can be inspired during many of the practical activities as they aim to initiate discussion, promote verbal responses and stimulate question-and-answer sessions. Joining in with simple number rhymes and songs helps to promote an interest in language. Opportunities for the children to develop skills in reading and writing can also be linked to a wide variety of activities, such as naming models, reading number words and compiling counting books.

Opportunities to encourage knowledge and understanding of the world are offered throughout the book in activities that involve the children in recalling or recording observations, exploring outdoor environments and making close observations.

Physical development is encouraged in activities that involve the children in using their gross motor skills, for example, by moving around a floor map and obstacle courses, and by playing throwing and aiming games. Fine motor skills are developed in activities requiring manual dexterity, such as cooking and handling ICT equipment.

Several activities in this book can be used to inspire creative development, especially those that involve making or using different shapes, creating patterns and making 2-D or 3-D models. There are also ideas to help the children to create colourful displays and join in role-play.

Links with home

It is important to involve parents and carers as much as possible by establishing good communication and developing positive links between the children's home and your setting. Keep them in touch with themes that you plan to explore each term or half-term, and suggest ways in which they can contribute towards the topic, for example, by providing relevant objects or artefacts for an interactive display. Provide parents and carers with a list of number rhymes or songs that you will be introducing to the children and ask if they know of any other relevant number rhymes or songs to share with them, for example, songs from the past or from a different country. Create a 'parents' notice-board', displaying a copy of your timetable or daily routines. It could also show a copy of your planning web or a brief list showing the cluster of Early

© MARTYN CHILLMAID

Learning Goals that the children will be working towards during their activities. Help parents and carers to realise how much they can help their children at home during everyday conversations, games and practical activities.

If possible, show parents and carers the various play areas within your setting and explain that their children will be learning and reinforcing mathematical concepts through their play. For example, playing floor games, table-top games and board games will help them to develop ideas about counting, quantity and numeral recognition, and creating patterns will promote an awareness of 2-D and 3-D shapes.

If possible, organise regular sessions when parents and carers can visit your setting to see their children 'in action'. This will give them the opportunity to observe and appreciate the wide range of mathematical experiences that their children encounter during the Foundation Stage.

Play areas
The activities in this book provide a spread of ideas for the play areas that are found in most nurseries, pre-schools and Reception classes. The play areas include: Role-play, Stories and rhymes, Outdoor environment, Sand, Water, ICT and sound, Small-world play, Art and craft, Natural discovery, Construction, and Malleable and tactile materials.

Here are a few examples of activities from the book that cover these play areas:
■ Role-play: 'Where shall I sit?' (page 19), 'The toy stall' (page 35), 'Tea for two' (page 53) and 'Teddies' sleepover' (page 75)
■ Stories and rhymes: 'Rhyme-time floor track' (page 20), 'Seven dwarfs' (page 40), 'Jump and bump' (page 41) and 'In the woods' (page 73)
■ Outdoor environment: 'Hopscotch' (page 31), 'Out and about' (page 47) and 'Roll to the rhombus!' (page 69)
■ Sand: 'Step across!' (page 22) and 'Sand butterflies' (page 66)
■ Water: 'Floaters or sinkers?' (page 25), 'Floating bottles' (page 43) and
■ in disguise' (page 70)
■ ICT and sound: 'Age plaques' (page 29), 'Ten in a bed' (page 33), 'One more instrument' (page 49) and 'Hare and Tortoise' (page 74)
■ Small-world play: 'Multi-storey model' (page 30), 'Come aboard!' (page 42), 'The building site' (page 51) and 'I spy' (page 71)
■ Art and craft: 'Counting house' (page 26) and 'Trip, trap' (page 39)
■ Natural discovery: 'How many legs?' (page 32), 'Make a snake' (page 50) and 'Leafy puzzle' (page 63)
■ Construction: 'Block-bugs' (page 24) and 'Four-eyed monster' (page 46)
■ Malleable and tactile materials: 'Spotty biscuits' (page 28), 'Ten fat sausages' (page 48) and 'Cheese straws' (page 60).

Planning

Planning for a progression of ideas

The Foundation Stage is aimed at children aged three to five. It begins when a child enters nursery, pre-school or play school, and continues until the end of the Reception Year at Infant or Primary school. The Foundation Stage prepares children for learning in Key Stage 1 of the National Curriculum, which begins in Year 1.

The curriculum for the Foundation Stage aims to underpin all future learning. Planning for a progression of ideas, from the beginning through to the end of the Foundation Stage, is therefore essential.

The document *Curriculum Guidance for the Foundation Stage* (QCA) identifies 'Stepping Stones' of progress from age three towards the 'Early Learning Goals' at the end of the Foundation Stage. Careful planning will help to provide satisfactory coverage of these Stepping Stones and will ensure that each child has been offered the necessary experiences for them to progress steadily towards the Early Learning Goals in Mathematical development.

Planning for equal opportunities

Children enter their early years environment with a wide variety of needs and experiences. Practitioners must be constantly aware of the importance of meeting the diverse needs of young children in their setting and aim to help all children to reach their full potential. Planning for equal opportunities during the Foundation stage requires an understanding of issues, such as special educational needs, gender, disabilities and religious and cultural differences. These issues are as important in Mathematical development as they are in all the other Areas of Learning, and a variety of strategies can be introduced to help all children make the best possible progress. The ideas and strategies employed will always depend on the specific needs of individual children. The document *Curriculum Guidance for the Foundation Stage* details a range of ideas to help practitioners to address these issues appropriately. In brief, these ideas suggest that practitioners should aim to:

■ plan opportunities that build and extend the children's self-esteem and confidence

■ use a variety of teaching strategies to meet the needs of each child

■ motivate and support the children to encourage their concentration and involvement

■ establish an environment free from harassment, in which the

© ANGELA MAYNARD

contribution of all children is recognised and valued

■ use materials and resources that reflect the diversity of the children's needs within the group

■ plan challenging opportunities for more able children

■ monitor the children's progress and take action when appropriate, for example, providing additional adult support or contacting the relevant agencies.

Providing equal opportunities in Mathematical development for children with special needs, for example, might involve using textured numerals or large print for visually impaired children, or ensuring extra adult help is available to provide hand-over-hand support for children who have poor hand control. If possible, organise an interpreter for children whose first language is not English, or invite a relative in to provide one-to-one support. Gender issues can be addressed by encouraging girls and boys to take an active part in mathematical activities in all the play areas, whether it be cooking, construction, handling tools or using equipment associated with ICT.

More able children can be challenged in Mathematical development by offering extension ideas, such as using bigger numbers, larger quantities and finding 'new' solutions to mathematical problems. Less able children, or children who have missed mathematical opportunities in the past, will benefit from using and listening to mathematical language, as much as possible, during everyday situations, for example, 'more than', 'less than', 'count the number', 'bigger than', 'smaller than' and so on.

Long-, medium- and short-term planning

The reason for long-, medium- and short-term plans is to help to establish a developmental approach to learning. This is as important in Mathematical development as it is in all other Areas of Learning.

Long-term planning

Long-term plans show what you aim to cover in the curriculum over one year in the Foundation Stage. In Mathematical development, the plans should help you to ensure that activities relating to all three clusters of Early Learning Goals ('Numbers as labels and for counting', 'Calculating' and 'Shape, space and measures') will be covered sufficiently. The plans will also help you to create a balanced approach to Mathematical development over the year, so that the children are offered activities that provide continuity and progression through the Stepping Stones towards the Early Learning Goals. The long-term plans should also provide a list of topics or themes that you hope to cover over the year, or establish which seasonal ideas or religious festivals you aim to introduce each term or half-term throughout the year.

Medium-term planning

Medium-term plans show curriculum coverage during each term or half-term. These plans should be developed from the long-term plans and will help you to establish which set of number skills and goals the children will be working towards during the term or half-term. These plans should also help you to think about how the activities can be adapted to suit different groups of children, for example, younger and older groups of children. Mathematical opportunities can also be linked to the particular topic, seasonal theme or festival that you plan to cover during the term or half-term. A seasonal theme on 'Growth', for example, would link well to mathematical activities such as measuring.

Short-term planning

Short-term plans provide a detailed outline of activities for each week or each day. To create an effective short-term plan of activities for individuals or groups of children in the Foundation Stage, a good knowledge of the children is necessary. Important information can be gathered from discussions with parents and carers and with other practitioners within your setting, but also from observations and assessments of the children. These discussions and observations can then be used to help your team to plan suitable activities and experiences for the children.

Short-term plans should include a list of learning intentions, based on the Stepping Stones and the Early Learning Goals, relevant to each child's stage of development in Mathematical development, as well as support and extension ideas. The plans could also include practical issues such as the type of mathematical resources required for each activity, when extra adult assistance is necessary and which play area is to be used. Plans should cater for children with special needs and for children of different ages and abilities.

It is sometimes useful to include timings on short-term plans, so that all the educators in your setting will know, for example, when to organise specific resources or play areas. You may also want to write a list of the names of the children to be included in each activity – this will ensure that the children who are absent or need reinforcement can do the activity at a later date. The lists can also help you to organise which children need to progress on to the next stage and will therefore provide a very useful record for future planning and assessments.

Organisation

Successful organisation derives from teamwork and shared planning. All adults working with the children on a regular basis should have an input and a clear understanding of the organisation and plans for your setting. Regular meetings can be used to evaluate the effectiveness of the plans and to discuss changes or extensions that need to be made to suit the needs of all the children. A key-worker system can be a very useful way of making sure that every child is acknowledged when plans and organisational issues are discussed. A key-worker system means that every child is supervised by a particular adult who monitors their achievements, records their progress and is available to report to the rest of the team regarding specific observations or needs of the child. The way that records are kept should be consistent, and these should be updated regularly by all key workers.

Practical organisation of your setting is very important to create an environment where everyone has a clear knowledge of the resources available and where they are stored. It is useful to have a visual plan of where the play areas are in each room, and a list of resources required within each area. These visual plans and lists can then be revised according to the theme or topics being covered each week, term or half-term.

Play areas
Any early years setting should have suitable play areas and a numeracy-rich environment for Mathematical development. The following list provides a few suggestions for planning ongoing activities and resources for each of the main play areas.

Role-play
■ Label each dressing-up box with a list of contents, for example, '3 tops, 4 wigs and 2 boots'. Alternatively, use pictures instead of words to describe the items.

■ Write a selection of door numbers or number words for the children to hang on to the playhouse door.
■ Label commercial or child-made puppets with numbers, and keep them in the role-play area for the children to name and use for spontaneous plays about number characters, for example, 'Mr Nine', 'Sally Six' and 'Eddie Eight'.

Stories and rhymes
■ Read to the children and display a selection of traditional story-books that refer to a particular number of characters or that use mathematical language, for example, 'The Three Billy Goats Gruff', 'The Three Little Pigs', 'The Enormous Turnip' and 'Goldilocks and the Three Bears' (Traditional).
■ Sing counting songs and rhymes with the children, such as 'Ten Fat Sausages', 'Five Little Frogs' and 'There Were Ten in the Bed' (Traditional).
■ Make a selection of big books illustrating the children's favourite counting rhymes. Display the books in the reading corner or library area.

Outdoor environment

■ Place number buckets or baskets in the outdoor play area for the children to use in throwing and aiming games.
■ Chalk a number ladder, a 'Hopscotch' pattern or a small number square on the playground or patio area for games involving hopping, skipping and jumping.
■ Paint giant numbers on the playground, or hang a large number line along a fence for the children to use as parking spaces for their pedal cars and bikes.

Sand

■ Store a selection of paper flags, showing numbers or dots, near the sand tray for the children to place on sand-castles.
■ Keep an assortment of interesting objects near the sand-pit for the children to bury, find and count.
■ Provide a selection of plastic or wooden numbers and a large dice to inspire matching and sorting games in the sand.

© DIGITAL VISION LTD

Water

■ Put together a store of different-sized plastic containers, such as tall narrow pots and wide shallow dishes, for the children to fill up, pour and compare.
■ Collect an assortment of plastic objects for the children to 'fish' and count.
■ Place a tub of plastic numerals near to the water tray for the children to retrieve and identify.

ICT and sound

■ Label containers with shape pictures to store musical instruments. For example, a container showing a picture of a circle could be used to store cymbals, a picture of a cylinder could refer to drums and scrapers and so on.
■ Place numbers on the keys of a tape recorder, for example, 1 for 'Play' and 2 for 'Stop'.
■ Place numbers on the keys of an electronic keyboard for the children to follow in order to create a simple tune. Change the position of the numbers on a regular basis so that the children have new tunes to play.

Small-world play

■ Write number figures or number words on roads, car parks or platforms on commercial or child-made playmats for the children to refer to during imaginative play.
■ Paint numbers on to toy vehicles and encourage the children to use the numbers as they play, for example, 'I'm going to drive train number 7' or 'Let's follow bus number 4'.
■ Provide accessories for soft-toy pets, for example, pretend leads made from wide ribbon in different lengths, or cardboard-box beds in different sizes. Encourage the children to use mathematical language as they play, to compare the different-sized accessories.

© DIGITAL STOCK

Art and craft
■ Invite the children to help to paint, print or make collages of resources for ongoing displays, for example, number friezes, number mobiles and number tracks.
■ Write words or draw pictures to describe the size of paintbrushes to be stored in certain containers, for example, 'big', 'small', 'long', 'short', 'fat' and 'thin'.

Natural discovery
■ Display a selection of different types of weighing scales for the children to use on a regular basis during their play situations, for example, in the home corner, the cooking area and the sand tray.
■ Keep a store of magnets for the children to experiment with, and for them to use to make simple games.
■ Provide seasonal books and posters that relate to objects and artefacts that the children are likely to bring in from home or from explorations outside. Encourage the children to use the books and posters as a simple reference library to compare the shapes, sizes and patterns of their findings, for example, leaves, flowers, stones and feathers.

Construction
■ Take photographs of models and patterns made by the children using bricks and blocks such as LEGO and DUPLO. Display these pictures in the construction area as a resource of ideas and to encourage observational skills by posing problems such as, 'Find a model that is made with six bricks', 'Which pattern uses squares?', 'How many circles are there in this picture?', 'Can you find a picture where there are rectangles?' and so on.
■ Help the children to create scenery boards, for example, a garden path, an underwater scene or a treasure island. Encourage them to use positional language, such as 'behind' and 'next to', as they move their models around the scenes.
■ Provide separate boxes or drawstring bags for different-sized bricks, for example, a small bag or box for small bricks, a middle-sized bag or box for middle-sized bricks, and so on.

Malleable and tactile materials
■ Help the children to make and display a number line using a variety of textured materials.
■ Encourage the children to make 3-D number shapes using clay or salt dough. Invite them to use the shapes for matching and sorting activities or for an interactive display.
■ Create a feely bag by placing one to ten different-textured items or different-shaped objects in a drawstring bag. Hang the bag in a prominent position and invite the children to count the number of objects by touching them. Change the number of objects in the bag on a regular basis.

Mathematical development

Assessment

The importance of assessment

It is important for early years practitioners to use assessment during the Foundation Stage for a variety of reasons, for example:

- to ensure effective coverage of the Stepping Stones and Early Learning Goals for Mathematical development
- to monitor and record the children's progress
- to help to plan activities that cater for the needs of the children
- to ascertain if, or when, support or extension activities are required
- to provide other practitioners, agencies, parents and carers with a clear picture of each child's attainments.

© ANGELA MAYNARD

Assessment, when completed carefully, can offer practitioners a comprehensive view of each child's mathematical development during the Foundation Stage. The assessment procedure can also be used to check that the Stepping Stones and Early Learning Goals are being covered adequately. For example, if the assessment results show that a child is having trouble understanding certain skills within one of the clusters, reinforcement activities can be introduced before embarking on new skills within the same cluster.

Assessment is a useful tool when monitoring the progress of individual children. It can be used as an aid to planning by providing information about the mathematical needs and achievements of individuals or groups of children. Activities can be planned or reviewed according to the assessment results, and appropriate support or extension activities can be introduced. Assessment can also alert practitioners to children that may have special educational needs, for example, particular strengths or weaknesses. Assessment results, in such cases, can provide evidence that would be useful to the appropriate support groups, other practitioners and parents or carers.

Methods of assessment

There are two main methods of assessing the children's needs and progress during the Foundation Stage: informal assessment and formal assessment.

Informal assessment

When the children have settled into their setting, the first assessments can be made. The results of these assessments will provide a picture of the children's mathematical abilities on entering the setting. Assessments at this early stage are likely to be informal observations made during the children's play activities. Parents and carers can also provide valuable information about their children's experiences at home – for example, some children might be extremely competent at using a particular

program on a home computer, while other children might have a rich knowledge of counting rhymes. These first informal observations and discussions can help practitioners to create a suitable plan of activities for each child or group of children using the appropriate Stepping Stones and Early Learning Goals as a starting-point.

Informal assessment should then continue as the children progress through the Foundation Stage to provide an ongoing record of each child's mathematical development. The activities in this book cover all the Early Learning Goals for Mathematical development, thus providing a comprehensive range of informal assessment opportunities for all three clusters.

Formal assessment

Opportunities for formal assessment need to be identified and planned in advance. Long-term plans, for example, could highlight assessment opportunities during the course of one year, such as one assessment at the end of each term, or the first assessment at the beginning of the year, followed by the second assessment in the middle of the year and the final assessment at the end of the year. Medium-term plans could ensure that there is an even spread of assessment opportunities covering each cluster of goals. Short-term plans could identify specific Stepping Stones or Early Learning Goals to be assessed, and the children and key workers involved in the assessment. The number of assessments should remain manageable and the style of the activity should be familiar to the children.

Opportunities for assessment

Mathematical development occurs gradually as children become confident and competent in learning and using key skills such as sorting, matching, counting, pattern-finding, pattern-making, number recognition and an awareness of shape, space and measures. Opportunities for assessing these skills should be sought during activities familiar in any early years environment, for example, games, imaginative play, construction play, handling of malleable materials, drawing, printing and model-making. All children need to be given the best opportunities for

© DIGITAL STOCK

developing their mathematical skills, and this includes providing the best opportunities for them to succeed during assessment procedures.

Children need activities that stimulate their interest, and this is also true when they are given assessment tasks. Each child's full potential is far more likely to shine through if they enjoy the activity or assessment.

© DIGITAL STOCK

Gathering evidence

There are two main forms of record-keeping that can be used to monitor and assess the children's needs and progress during the Foundation Stage:

■ records completed by the practitioner or key worker, for example, informal records such as observation notes, and formal, ongoing records such as the assessment sheets that you can find on pages 79–81 in this book, as well as other formal assessments to be carrried out throughout the Foundation Stage.

■ a portfolio of the children's work containing examples of the children's drawings, written work and activity sheets, along with photographic records showing examples of the children's 2-D and 3-D constructions and models.

Using the assessment sheets

The photocopiable assessment sheets on pages 79–81 in this book are based on the targets prescribed by the QCA which broadly reflect the Early Learning Goals and Stepping Stones. They provide a complete list of the Early Learning Goals for the three clusters and can be used to record the children's progress in Mathematical development throughout the duration of the Foundation Stage. There is room for you to make notes and comments as you observe each child at play.

Foundation Stage Profile

In January 2003, the Qualifications and Curriculum Authority introduced a new assessment document for early years practitioners working within the Foundation Stage. The *Foundation Stage Profile* provides a 12-page document to be completed for each child throughout the Foundation Stage. Within it the curriculum is broken down to provide assessment for all six Areas of Learning. For the Area of Mathematical development, there are 27 'targets'.

Practitioners will be expected to use their usual techniques of observation and occasional note-taking to gather evidence of the children's skills and abilities.

Using the photocopiable sheets for assessment

The following activities provide examples of how assessment procedures can fit easily into the familiar routines of the early years environment. They can also be used to provide a starting-point for practitioners who are new to assessment procedures during the Foundation Stage.

'Six snug teddy bears' (page 38)

■ Cluster: Numbers as labels and for counting.

■ Early Learning Goal: Say and use number names in order in familiar contexts.

■ Assessment procedure: Make five copies of the photocopiable sheet on page 85 to create ten separate teddy pictures. Label the teddies' nightcaps with numbers 1 to 10 or 0 to 9. Encourage the children to say the numbers on the nightcaps and to place the pictures in the correct order.

■ Note the numbers that each child can say and use in order.

'Seven dwarfs' (page 40)

■ Cluster: Calculating.

■ Early Learning Goal: In practical activities and discussion begin to use the vocabulary involved in adding and subtracting.

© FIONA PRAGOFF

■ Assessment procedure: Make a copy of the photocopiable sheet on page 87 and cut it into seven separate pictures. Place these in a row along the top of a rectangle of fabric to represent seven dwarfs in a bed. Remove the pictures one at a time to show that the dwarfs are getting out of bed and going to work. Talk with the children about the activity and encourage language such as 'take away', 'remove', 'one less', 'subtract' and 'minus'. Repeat the activity by inviting the children to put the dwarfs back into bed, encouraging language such as 'one more', 'add one' and 'another'.

■ Make a note of the vocabulary used by each child.

'Round the garden' (page 52)

■ Cluster: Shape, space and measures.

■ Early Learning Goal: Use everyday words to describe position.

■ Assessment procedure: Make a copy of the photocopiable sheet on page 89 and cut it into eight separate pictures. Arrange some or all of the pictures in a variety of positions, for example, one teddy hopping in between two teddies clapping, or three teddies sitting next to three teddies clapping. Ask the children to describe the different positions of the teddies.

■ Make a note of the words used by each child to describe position, for example, 'beside', 'above', 'next to', 'in between', 'under', 'a row' and so on.

Mathematical development

The activities in this chapter focus on the cluster 'Numbers as labels and for counting'. This includes saying and using number names in order, counting reliably up to ten objects, recognising numerals 1 to 9 and developing mathematical methods to solve practical problems.

Where shall I sit?

What to do
■ Help the children to write the numerals 1 to 5 on to ten rectangles of card to create five theatre tickets for play and five theatre seat numbers.
■ Invite the children to tape the seat numbers in numerical order along a row of five chairs in front of the puppet theatre and to place the theatre tickets in a bag or box.
■ Encourage the children to pick a ticket from the box and to find the seat with the matching number.
■ When all the children are seated, invite them to call out their ticket numbers, starting with the child in seat number 1.
■ Ask the children if they are seated in numerical order. If not, help them to find the correct seats.
■ Repeat the activity by inviting the children to select a different ticket.
■ Finally, encourage the children to use the role-play area for spontaneous puppet shows, using hand or stick puppets.
■ Help younger children to identify each number by drawing dots on to the tickets and seat labels.
■ Challenge older children by hiding one of the tickets. Help them to identify the missing ticket number by observing the number on the empty seat.

More ideas
■ Use tickets and seats labelled 1 to 10.
■ Create a different role-play setting, for example, an aeroplane or a bus.

Other curriculum areas
PD Place the numbered tickets next to five PE mats, in a large room. Encourage the children to become imaginary puppets, hopping, skipping or dancing around the room, crossing each mat in numerical order.
CD Invite the children to paint large colourful numbers to hang, in numerical order, across the back of the theatre seats.

Goals for the **Foundation Stage**

Stepping Stone
Show an interest in numbers and counting.

Early Learning Goal
Say and use number names in order in familiar contexts.

■

Group size
Five children.

■

What you need
Five chairs; commercial puppet theatre (or a low table draped with a colourful cloth); hand or stick puppets; ten small rectangles of card; pens; sticky tape; small box or bag.

Home links
Provide each child with five or ten small rectangles of card. Ask parents and carers to help their children to write the numbers 1 to 5 or 1 to 10 on the strips of card to create play tickets for imaginative play at home.

Rhyme-time floor track

Enjoy joining in with number rhymes and songs.

Early Learning Goal
Say and use number names in order in familiar contexts.

Group size
Five children.

What you need
Ten sheets of coloured A4 card, cut into simple footprint shapes; thick felt-tipped pens; five sheets of white A4 card; paints; painting equipment; laminator or sticky-backed plastic (optional).

Home links
Send home the photocopiable sheet 'One, two, buckle my shoe' on page 82 to encourage the children to say and use number names at home.

What to do

■ Sing or say the rhyme 'One, Two, Buckle My Shoe' (Traditional) with the children.
■ Help the children to label the ten card footprint shapes 1 to 10.
■ Next, provide each child with a sheet of white A4 card.
■ Allocate each child a picture to paint on to their card. The pictures should relate to the rhyme, for example, a shoe, a door, sticks, a gate and a hen.
■ When the pictures are dry, laminate them as well as the footprints, or cover them with sticky-backed plastic.

■ Help the children to sort the ten footprints in order along the floor to create a number track.
■ Scatter the five picture cards randomly around the footprints.
■ Encourage one of the children to step two spaces along the number track, while everyone chants the words 'One, two, buckle my shoe'. Then ask the children which picture should go after footprint number 2.
■ When the appropriate picture has been selected and positioned after the number 2, continue by chanting the words 'Three, four, knock at the door', and so on until all five pictures are included in the number track.
■ Scatter the pictures again and repeat the rhyme until all the children have taken a turn on the number track
■ For younger children, decorate each footprint with one to ten dots.
■ Help older children to write the number words, one to ten, on the footprints.

More ideas

■ Use the footprints without the pictures for activities involving counting on and counting back.
■ Provide a large dice, and real boots as counters, to inspire humorous number games. Encourage the children to take turns to move the boots.

Other curriculum areas

CD Help the children to create a colourful number track using real footprints or shoe prints.

CLL Introduce other number rhymes that can be used to encourage an awareness of numerical order, for example, 'Five Currant Buns', 'There Were Ten in the Bed' and 'Five Speckled Frogs' (Traditional).

Mathematical development

Ten pretty flowers

What to do

■ Place a different-coloured paint in each shallow container for printing.

■ Ask the children to select one or more sponge shapes to print a row or circle of five to ten colourful flowers on to a strip of pale-green card.

■ Leave to dry.

■ Invite the children to cut out a few simple leaf shapes from green sticky paper to decorate around their flowers.

■ Next, provide five to ten white or pale-yellow paper discs for the children to stick in the centre of each flower.

■ Encourage each child to create a floral number strip by writing numbers, in order, along the discs. Support them as necessary.

■ Help the children to write 'Start' in front of the first flower, and 'Finish' after the last flower.

■ When complete, provide the children with a dice and counters to use with their number strip to inspire counting games.

■ For younger children, provide pre-numbered discs for them to place in the correct order along their row of flowers.

■ Encourage older children to create a number strip showing up to 15 or 20 flowers.

More ideas

■ Introduce two dice for addition and subtraction activities.

■ Invite the children to cut out their own simple sponge shapes, to create a number strip with a different theme, for example, a row of kites, balloons or spiders.

Other curriculum areas

CLL Help the children to print, draw or paint a number strip with speech bubbles pointing to some of the numbers, for example, 'Go back 1 space', 'Move on 2 spaces', 'Miss a turn' and so on.

PSED Encourage the children to play number games in small groups to inspire turn-taking, co-operation and patience.

Stepping Stone
Willingly attempt to count, with some numbers in the correct order.

Early Learning Goal
Say and use number names in order in familiar contexts.

Group size
Small groups.

What you need
Thick paint in various bright colours; sponges cut into simple shapes to represent flowers (approximately 10cm wide); shallow containers; strips of pale-green card (approximately A4 or A3 size); sticky paper in shades of green; white or pale-yellow sticky paper discs (3 to 5cm wide); scissors; felt-tipped pens; glue sticks; dice; counters.

Home links
Ask parents and carers to encourage their children to count items as they set the table or put away the shopping.

Step across!

Stepping Stone
Say the number after any number up to 9.

Early Learning Goal
Say and use number names in order in familiar contexts.

Group size
Up to four children.

What you need
A sand tray; nine large stones numbered 1 to 9; toy watering can; small plastic characters and accessories (trees, flowers, shells, large colourful beads and so on); old wooden brick labelled with 1 on four sides and 0 on two sides to make a dice; small LEGO house.

Home links
Help the children to make a simple number line to take home and cut into individual numbers for reassembling in the correct order.

What to do
■ Invite the children to say the numbers on the stones and to lay them, in order, across the sand tray. Then place the LEGO house after stone number 9.

■ Encourage the children to use the small-world accessories from your selection to create a colourful garden scene. Each child should then place one toy character in front of stone number 1.

■ Now, add an element of surprise by sprinkling a little water on to the scene!

Explain to the children that they are going to play a game to try to get their characters across the stones and to the house before a thunderstorm arrives!

■ Ask the first player to throw the dice. If 1 is shown, the character can be moved one step. If 0 is shown, the character cannot be moved and the dice is passed on to the next player.

■ Ask the children questions such as, 'Which number is on the next stone?', 'What number comes after 4?' and so on.

■ When the winner reaches the house, use the watering can to create a downpour!

■ With younger children, begin by using five stones.

■ Encourage older children to help you to write or paint the numbers on to the stones.

Other curriculum areas
KUW Take the children outside to count, sort and order natural objects, for example, sticks, flowers, feathers and so on.

PD Introduce traditional playground games such as 'Hopscotch'.

More ideas
■ Invite the children to create nine 'toadstools' by drawing one to nine red spots on to nine discs of white card taped on to nine cotton reels. Encourage the children to place them in numerical order, across the sand tray.

■ Help the children to use sand and glue to create textured number cards for sorting, ordering and matching.

Textured numbers

What to do
■ Help each child to draw a horizontal line across the centre of a sheet of card and to use one or two large number templates to draw a number between 1 and 15 above the line.
■ Encourage the children to decorate inside their number shapes using their choice of textured materials.

■ Ask each child to say the number that is on their sheet of card. If the number is 8, for example, help them to select eight small textured objects or to cut eight random shapes from textured materials, and invite them to stick these beneath the horizontal line.
■ When 15 sheets of card have been decorated, encourage the children to help you to compile them into numerical order, 1 to 15.
■ Secure the number cards together using a hole-punch and ribbon to create a 15-page big book.

■ Use the big book to inspire an interest in counting beyond ten and to help number recognition.
■ For younger children, provide 15 sheets of card already prepared with the horizontal line and the number shapes 1 to 15.
■ Invite older children to create a big book showing even numbers up to 20 for counting in twos.

More ideas
■ Invite the children to manipulate clay, Plasticine or salt dough into 3-D number shapes. Encourage them to place two shapes together to create numbers beyond ten. Ask each child to say their number to the rest of the group.
■ Organise a number hunt by hiding a series of number cards around the room, or within a safe outdoor area. Encourage the children to find the numbers and to place them in the correct order.

Other curriculum areas
PD Play throwing and aiming games using more than ten different objects. Then help the children to count, for example, how many beanbags landed in a hoop, balls in a box and so on.
KUW Encourage the children to count out more than ten components from a construction kit to build a structure that is tall, long or wide.

Stepping Stone
Begin to count beyond 10.

Early Learning Goal
Say and use number names in order in familiar contexts.
■
Group size
Small groups.
■
What you need
A variety of textured collage materials (shiny fabric, corduroy, bumpy wallpaper, bubble wrap, glitter and so on); 15 sheets of A3 card; large number templates 0 to 9 (approximately A4 or A5 size); glue; hole-punch; ribbon; scissors.

Home links
Ask parents and carers to contribute resources for the big book. Encourage the children to help you to sort and count the items.

Mathematical development

Block-bugs

What to do
■ Provide 19 large construction blocks.
■ Invite the children to secure a pair of bug eyes and two pipe-cleaner antennae on to ten of the blocks, to create ten imaginary creatures called 'Block-bugs'.
■ Next, invite the children to give three of the Block-bugs an extra block (see diagram).
■ Then ask the children to give three other Block-bugs an extra two blocks.
■ Invite the children to place all ten bugs on the floor to play a game.
■ Encourage them to take turns to remove a numbered ball or brick from the bag. If the number 1 is shown, the child should select a bug constructed from one block; if 2 is shown, they should choose a two-block bug, and if 3 is shown, a three-block bug.
■ The ball or brick is then replaced into the bag and the next player takes their turn. If there are no bugs left to match the number shown, the player misses a turn.
■ This process continues until all the bugs have been removed. The winner is the player with the most bugs.
■ With younger children, use bugs consisting of only one or two construction blocks and a bag containing only the numbers 1 and 2.
■ Invite older children to find a winner to each game by counting how many blocks they have acquired instead of how many bugs.

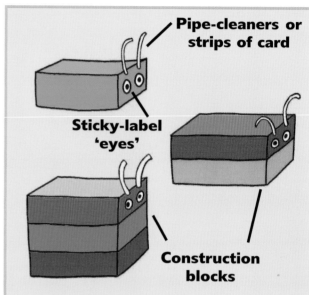

Pipe-cleaners or strips of card

Sticky-label 'eyes'

Construction blocks

More ideas
■ Encourage the children to place groups of one, two or three soft toys in baskets, on shelves or on chairs.
■ Help the children to place the correct number of beads or buttons into the compartments of a numbered sorting tray.

Other curriculum areas
PSED Encourage the children to form into groups of two or three for movement activities.

PD Encourage a small group of children to count and share ten dressing-up items that they use for role-play.

Floaters or sinkers?

What to do
■ Provide the children with a collection of objects that float and sink. Encourage them to predict which objects will float. Then help them to test their predictions by placing a small group of objects in the water tray.
■ Ask questions such as, 'How many objects have sunk?', 'Are more than two floating?', 'How many objects are there altogether?' and so on.
■ Invite the children to choose a selection of materials to make a simple boat, for example, a block of wood for the hull, paper for the sails and a straw for the mast.
■ When the boats are made, encourage the children to place them in the water tray.
■ Ask questions to encourage the children to count groups of boats, for example, 'How many boats are on the water?', 'How many boats have sunk?', 'Are there more than two boats with red sails?' and so on.
■ Help younger children during the construction stage.
■ Encourage older children to recognise groups of four or five boats.

More ideas
■ Challenge the children to count boats while they are moving.
■ Tie a cord across the top of a water tray to divide it into two sections. Place groups of one, two or three toy boats in each section for the children to count and compare.

Other curriculum areas
CD Say the rhyme 'Rub-a-dub-dub' (Traditional). Then invite the children to draw or paint a picture showing three tubs, the first holding one man, the second, two men and the third, three men.
CLL Encourage the children to join in with the words of the rhyme 'One, Two, Three, Four, Five' (Traditional). Ask five or ten children to hold ten paper fish, secured to lengths of thread as props for counting.

Stepping Stone
Count up to three or four objects by saying one number name for each item.

Early Learning Goal
Count reliably up to 10 everyday objects.
■
Group size
Small groups.
■
What you need
Water tray; collection of materials that float or sink, such as small blocks of wood, foil containers, strips of polystyrene, corks, cotton reels, stones and so on; construction materials such as plastic straws, cocktail sticks, lolly sticks, small swatches of paper, fabric, card, insulating tape or sticky tape and Blu-Tack or play dough; scissors.

Home links
Ask parents and carers to encourage their children to find up to ten tiny items to place in an empty matchbox.

Counting house

Stepping Stone
Count out up to six objects from a larger group.

Early Learning Goal
Count reliably up to 10 everyday objects.

Group size
Small groups.

What you need
A copy or knowledge of the rhyme 'Sing a Song of Sixpence' (Traditional); ten round card cheese boxes; shiny paper or foil; glue; strips of colourful card (long enough to fit around a child's head); crayons or coloured sticky paper; tray; table.

What to do
■ Sing the rhyme 'Sing a Song of Sixpence' with the children and explain that they are going to make their own coins.
■ Allow a high degree of independence as the children decorate round boxes using shiny paper to create ten 'coins'.
■ Provide each child with a strip of card to decorate using crayons or paper shapes. When the children have completed their strips, help them to bend and tape them into crowns, to wear as they pretend to be the king counting his coins.
■ Place all the coins on a tray. Invite one child at a time to count out six coins to put on the table in front of them. Ask them to put the coins in a straight line and to count them again. Then encourage them to put the coins in a circle and count them once more.

■ Invite the children to think of other arrangements for their sets of six coins. Ask questions such as, 'How many coins are there in the line?', 'Are there still six coins if they are placed in a circle?' and so on.
■ Encourage younger children to count out a smaller quantity of coins.
■ Invite older children to count and arrange up to ten coins.

More ideas
■ Provide other items for the children to count while pretending to be the king in his counting house, for example, colourful beads, jewellery and play banknotes.
■ Invite the children to stick one to six shiny paper coins on to several sheets of card cut into the shape of a purse. Display the purses for the children to compare quantities.

Home links
Ask parents and carers to play simple shop games with their children using real one-penny coins for counting, buying and selling items.

Other curriculum areas
PSED Encourage the children to count out and share cakes made in your setting.

CD Invite the children to draw or paint one to ten blackbirds on to round sheets of paper to represent birds in a pie. Use a row of pictures to create an interesting counting frieze based on the rhyme 'Sing a Song of Sixpence'.

Mathematical development

Five coloured flags

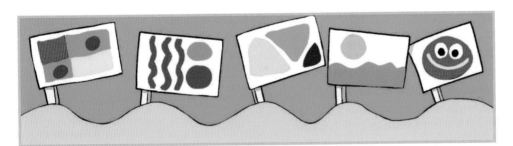

Stepping Stone
Count actions or objects that cannot be moved.

Early Learning Goal
Count reliably up to 10 everyday objects.

Group size
Five children.

What you need
A sand tray containing damp sand; five lolly sticks; five rectangles of paper (approximately 5cm x 7cm); colourful pens; sticky tape; small spade; small buckets or plastic cups.

What to do

■ Provide each child with a rectangle of paper to decorate and tape on to a lolly stick to create a flag.

■ Invite the children to make five sand-castles or mounds in the sand tray, one for each flag.

■ Ask the children to count the flags without touching them. Check that they count each flag once and that they count all the flags in the group.

■ Sing the following song with the children to the tune of 'Five Currant Buns' (Traditional):

Five coloured flags lined up in the sand,
Tall and proud and looking very grand.
Along came (child's name) with a spade one day,
Dug up a coloured flag and took it right away.

At this point, the named child should dig up the first flag.

■ Continue singing the rhyme, counting the flags between each verse. Ask questions such as, 'How many flags are there?', 'Two have gone away, how many are left?', 'How many flags are missing?' and so on.

■ For younger children, provide flags with numbers on. Each time a flag is to be removed, make sure that the child takes away the flag with the biggest number.

■ Encourage older children to say the numerical sum between each verse, for example, five flags take away one flag leaves four flags.

More ideas

■ Invite the children to sing 'Dug up two coloured flags' instead of just one flag, then to count down by two each verse.

■ Extend the song to 'Ten coloured flags'.

Other curriculum areas

KUW Take the children on a nature walk and count items that cannot be touched, for example, trees in a garden, birds on the grass and ducks on a pond.

CD Invite the children to paint bold pictures of things that can be seen in the air, for example, kites, balloons, birds and planes. Display the pictures up high and out of reach, for the children to count without touching.

Home links
Encourage parents and carers to ask their children to count objects while on their journey home, for example, windows on houses, children in the park and babies in prams.

Spotty biscuits

Stepping Stone
Count an irregular arrangement of up to 10 objects.

Early Learning Goal
Count reliably up to 10 everyday objects.

Group size
Small groups.

What you need
Ingredients: 225g self-raising flour; 150g butter; 100g castor sugar; 1 egg; pinch of salt; chocolate drops. Equipment: sieve; bowl; shaped cutters; baking tray; board; cooking facilities (adult use); hand-washing facilities; clean aprons.

Preparation
Check for any food allergies or dietary requirements.

What to do
■ Pre-heat the oven.
■ Make sure that the children wash their hands and that each wears an apron.
■ Help the children to sift the flour and salt into a bowl. Rub in the butter. Add the sugar, then the egg, and mix to a dough. Knead it until it is smooth, then roll out the mixture on to a floured board.
■ Invite the children to cut out ten or more biscuit shapes with shaped cutters, and to place them on a baking tray.

■ Ask questions such as, 'How many shapes are on the tray?', 'If we add two more shapes, how many will there be?', 'Can you find ten shapes?' and so on.
■ Encourage the children to put one to five chocolate drops on to each biscuit shape.
■ Ask questions such as, 'How many shapes have three chocolate drops?', 'Can you find two shapes with the same number of chocolate drops?', 'Which shapes have less than four chocolate drops?' and so on.
■ Set the oven to 180°C/350°F/Gas Mark 4 and bake the biscuits for ten to 12 minutes.
■ When the biscuits are cool, invite the children to eat them or take them home.
■ With younger children, work in pairs rather than in groups.
■ Invite older children to help you to weigh the ingredients.

More ideas
■ Encourage the children to count irregular arrangements of everyday items, for example, food inside a lunch box, jigsaw pieces and toys on the floor.
■ Ask the children to count objects that move, for example, children playing, fish in a tank and toy trains on a track.

Other curriculum areas
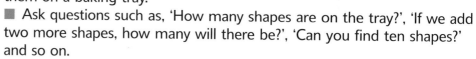
CD Invite the children to draw or paint one to ten spots on to light-brown discs of paper to represent giant biscuits. Hang them back to back to create interesting mobiles for counting and comparing.
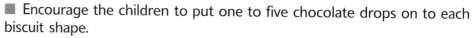
PD Use the game of 'Skittles' to challenge the children to count irregular arrangements of objects.

Home links
Ask parents and carers to encourage their children to count items in picture books and nursery-rhyme books during story time at home.

Age plaques

What to do
■ Set up an art package on a computer and show the children how to create colourful patterns on the screen.
■ Print out each child's design.
■ Next, provide ten large templates showing the numbers 0 to 9 and ask the children which number matches their age.

■ Help each child to draw around the appropriate template on to black card and to cut out the number shape.
■ Encourage the children to position their number shape in the centre of their colourful printout using several thick sticky pads so that it appears to stand proud of the background.
■ Mount each child's work on to black paper or card, and label it with their name to create an unusual age plaque.

■ Display the age plaques on the wall and use them to inspire use of mathematical language by asking questions such as, 'How many children are five?', 'Who will be six next birthday?', 'Are there more children who are four, five or six?' and so on.
■ Ensure that younger children place the sticky pads on the reverse side of the card number shapes.
■ Encourage older children to create pictures using the art package.

More ideas
■ Help the children to identify and write other numbers of personal significance, such as house numbers, birthday dates and siblings' ages.
■ Play 'Missing number' games using a puppet and a number track. Ask questions such as, 'Which number is hidden under the puppet?'.

Other curriculum areas
PSED Invite the children to design a birthday card, badge or bookmark for someone special, showing the person's age or birth date on the front.

CD Help the children to use marbling inks to create a colourful background for a number line showing raised black numerals 0 to 9. Ask them to identify significant numbers.

Stepping Stone
Recognise some numerals of personal significance.

Early Learning Goal
Recognise numerals 1 to 9.

Group size
Individuals, or pairs of children.

What you need
Computer; colour printer; A4 paper; art package such as *Splosh* (Kudlian); black paper or thin card; double-sided thick sticky pads; large number templates (approximately A5 size); scissors.

Home links
Provide each child with a strip of card, divided into ten equal spaces, to take home to create a number line to reinforce number recognition and number writing skills.

Multi-storey model

What to do
■ Provide the children with three or four boxes and some toy vehicles.
■ Help them to tape the boxes, one on top of the other, to represent a multi-storey car park. Tape this to a wall or cupboard. Let the children add strips of grey card to the model to create roads and ramps (see diagram).
■ Invite the children to draw lines, wide enough to fit the vehicles, inside each box to represent parking spaces.
■ Ask the children to write a number label for each space. Place the labels in numerical order or randomly.
■ Provide a smaller box for the children to decorate to represent a ticket booth. Then invite them to place a small-world person inside it to represent a car-park attendant.
■ Invite the children to write or draw other labels for the car park, for example, arrows, stop signs and 'No parking' signs.
■ Encourage the children to use the car park to play games involving finding and identifying numbered parking spaces.

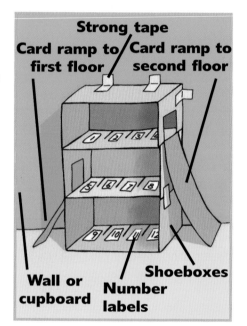

Strong tape
Card ramp to first floor / Card ramp to second floor
Wall or cupboard Number labels Shoeboxes

■ Introduce challenges such as, 'Can you park three cars in spaces showing the numbers 6, 7 and 8?'.
■ Ask younger children to make a car park using number labels 1 to 5.
■ Challenge older children to label parking spaces with numbers up to 20.

More ideas
■ Invite the children to draw numbers using a wide variety of tools and techniques, for example, in sand, using finger-paints and so on.
■ Set up a role-play area that inspires number recognition and number writing, for example, a post office or a travel agency.

Other curriculum areas
PD Help the children to mark out large numbers on a playground using coloured chalk. Encourage them to follow the numbers in the correct direction by skipping, jumping, walking and so on.

CLL Sing an adapted version of the rhyme 'Five Little Ducks' (Traditional) with the children: 'Five little cars drove out one day, Over the hills and far away, The biggest car said, "Hoot, hoot, hoot, hoot", But only four little cars came back.' Encourage the children to use their fingers to show the number of cars in each verse.

Mathematical development

Hopscotch

What to do

■ Provide the children with some chalk and invite them to write the numbers 1 to 5, or 1 to 9, on paving slabs outside, to create a traditional 'Hopscotch' track. Alternatively, draw a 'Hopscotch'-style grid on the ground to create a similar effect.

■ Encourage the children to take it in turns to spin the giant spinner, say the number that it lands on and hop or jump accordingly along the 'Hopscotch' track.

■ As the children play, ask questions such as, 'Which number have you landed on?', 'What number is next?', 'If you jump back one space, what number will you be standing on?' and so on.

■ The winner is the first child to hop or jump all the way to the end of the track and back again. Alternatively, just play for fun.

■ Help younger children to form their numbers correctly as they write them on the ground.

■ Encourage older children to create a 'Hopscotch' track using numbers up to 12.

More ideas

■ Draw a simple 'Hopscotch' track showing ten sections on to a sheet of A4 paper. Make a photocopy for each child. Help them to write the numerals 1 to 10 in the spaces and to use the track with a dice and counters to inspire simple number games.

■ Provide each child with an A4 card copy of the photocopiable sheet to colour in, cut out and use with the A4 'Hopscotch' game above.

Other curriculum areas

PSED Encourage turn-taking and co-operation while pairs or groups of children play traditional board games such as 'Snakes and ladders' and 'Ludo'.

CD Invite the children to use colourful paints or sticky paper squares to create a checked gameboard, decorated with fabric snakes and paper straw ladders.

Stepping Stone
Recognise numerals 1 to 5, then 1 to 9.

Early Learning Goal
Recognise numerals 1 to 9.

Group size
Any size.

What you need
An A3 copy of the photocopiable sheet 'Spinner' on page 83; strong tape, thick cardboard (approximately A3 size); scissors; dowelling rod (approximately 20cm long); coloured pencils; chalk; safe outdoor area.

Preparation
Glue the enlarged photocopy of the spinner on to thick cardboard. Neatly wrap the edges of the cardboard using strong tape. Colour each section on the giant spinner and place a dowelling rod through the centre.

Home links
Ask parents and carers to play traditional board games with their children to help to reinforce number recognition at home.

How many legs?

Select the correct numeral to represent 1 to 5, then 1 to 9, objects.

Early Learning Goal
Recognise numerals 1 to 9.

Group size
Five children.

What you need
An outdoor area where it is safe for children to observe minibeasts; magnifying glasses; five sheets of A4 or A3 paper; paints; painting equipment; 15 narrow strips of fabric or paper; sticky tape; long display area at the children's height; five pieces of card labelled 1 to 5 (approximately A5 size).

Home links
Ask parents and carers to help their children to cut out animal pictures from old magazines to bring in to your setting. Help the children to create a vibrant counting display showing, for example, one cat, two dogs and so on.

What to do
■ Take the children to a safe outdoor area to observe minibeasts in their natural habitat. Provide magnifying glasses and encourage the children to look for animals with no legs, a few legs and lots of legs.
■ Ask the children to talk about the animals that they observe and to describe their appearance.
■ Back indoors, provide each child with a sheet of A4 or A3 paper. Encourage them to use their creative imagination to paint an animal without legs. When the paintings are complete, display them in a line on the wall, at the children's height.
■ Provide the children with strips of colourful fabric or paper to represent legs. Invite the children to tape one leg on to the first painting, two on the second, and so on up to five legs on the last painting.
■ Show the children the number cards labelled 1 to 5. Point to one of the paintings and ask the children to select the correct number card to match the number of legs on the animal. Repeat this process for all five paintings.
■ Invite younger children to touch the legs as they count.
■ Encourage older children to paint nine imaginary animals with one to nine legs.

More ideas
■ Place the number cards next to the appropriate pictures, with two numbers in the wrong position. Ask the children to identify the mistake.
■ Place all the number cards in the wrong position for the children to rearrange.

Other curriculum areas
KUW Invite the children to construct 3-D creatures using interlocking bricks on which they can attach card or fabric legs to count and label.
CD Talk about real animals with two, four, six, eight and no legs.

Mathematical development

Ten in a bed

What to do

■ Provide each child with a blank counting strip. Encourage them to draw a smiley face in each of the ten spaces on the strip of card to represent ten dolls or teddies resting on ten pillows.

■ Invite the children to decorate the area below the smiley faces to represent a quilt or blanket, and above the faces to represent a bed's headboard.

■ Sing the rhyme 'There Were Ten in the Bed' with the children and as you go through it, encourage them to pull the strip of card so that one character at a time falls out of bed.

■ Ask the children to count between verses to check that they have the correct number of characters in the bed.

■ Continue this process until there are no faces left in the bed.

■ For younger children, make an enlarged version of the counting strip to use as a visual resource during group work.

■ Ask older children questions to inspire an awareness of counting on and counting back, for example, 'If four faces are in the bed and two more are added, how many are there altogether?' or 'If seven faces are in the bed and three fall out, how many are left?'.

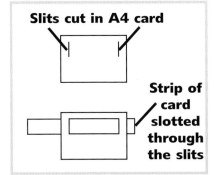

Slits cut in A4 card

Strip of card slotted through the slits

More ideas

■ Count dolls or teddies under a blanket.

■ Count the children as they mime the actions of the song.

Other curriculum areas

CD Invite the children to model ten Plasticine characters to sort and count.

PD Explore the theme of rolling by providing different-sized balls for the children to roll towards a target. Help the children to keep a numerical score as they play.

Stepping Stone
Use some number names accurately in play.

Early Learning Goal
Recognise numerals 1 to 9.

Group size
Small groups.

What you need
A sheet of A4 card for each child; a narrow strip of thick card for each child (approximately 5cm x 50cm); sharp scissors (adult use); coloured pens or pencils; copy or knowledge of the rhyme 'There Were Ten in the Bed' (Traditional).

Preparation
Cut two 5cm slits in a sheet of A4 card. Slot the narrow strip of card through the slits. Draw ten squares (approximately 2cm x 2cm) along the narrow strip to create a blank counting strip (see diagram).

Home links
Invite the children to take their counting strips home to use with their parents or carers.

The bus lane

Stepping Stone
Use some number names and number language spontaneously.

Early Learning Goal
Use developing mathematical ideas and methods to solve practical problems.

Group size
Small groups.

What you need
A copy or knowledge of the song 'The Wheels on the Bus' (Traditional); interlocking construction blocks such as Mega Blocks; card; sticky labels; pens; masking tape.

What to do
■ Sing the song 'The Wheels on the Bus' with the children.
■ Provide a range of construction blocks for the children to build several model buses that can be pushed along the floor, with or without functional wheels.
■ Give the children sticky labels and invite them to write numbers for the front of their buses.
■ Clear a route around the room to represent a bus lane. Use masking tape to secure signs such as 'Stop', 'Give way', 'Slow' and 'Bus stop'.
■ Ask the children to write number labels for the bus stops.
■ Suggest practical problems to encourage the children to use number names spontaneously while they manoeuvre the buses around the route, for example, bus number 2 has broken down, bus number 3 is lost, two buses are needed at bus stop number 4 and so on.
■ Invite younger children to play in pairs using three or four buses and a couple of bus stops.
■ Encourage older children to make up to six buses to manoeuvre between four to six bus stops.

More ideas
■ Label pedal vehicles with numbers for the children to ride outside around a series of numbered skittles (or other numbered obstructions). Encourage the children to talk about where they have ridden, where they are going and which vehicles they have used.
■ Provide a wide variety of opportunities for the children to count during play situations, for example, plates in the home corner, books on a shelf and so on.

Home links
Invite parents and carers in to listen to their children singing number rhymes and songs, including adapted versions of traditional songs.

Other curriculum areas
CD Invite the children to paint a row of buses. Help them to label these with even, odd or a sequence of numbers.
CLL Encourage the children to join in singing a new version of the song 'The Wheels on the Bus'. The first verse starts with the words 'Two wheels on a bike', the second verse with 'Four wheels on a car', then 'Six wheels on a lorry', and finally 'Eight wheels on a train'.

Mathematical development

The toy stall

What to do
■ Invite the children to display the toys on one table, and the till, money, pens, paper, notepads and other materials on another table.
■ Help the children to write price labels to attach to the toys, and signs such as 'Open', 'Closed', '2 for 1' and so on.
■ Encourage role-play situations involving practical problems such as identifying correct coins, sorting out money and giving change.
■ Show the children acting as stall holders how to write very simple receipts listing the prices of items sold, and how to use a calculator to add and total.

■ Help the children acting as customers to count how many pennies they have to spend and to check the amount of change that they receive.
■ Give younger children five to ten one-penny coins to count and spend.
■ Encourage older children to use a range of coins such as 1p, 2p, 5p and 10p.

More ideas
■ Invite the children to help you to make a simple sorting tray using shallow pots slotted into an open-edged cereal box. The different coins can be sorted into separate compartments during role-play.
■ Help the children to write a price list of the toys on the stall, to display in the role-play area, to stimulate mathematical language such as 'more than', 'less than', 'least', 'most' and so on.

Other curriculum areas
CD Invite the children to make simple stick puppets to sell in the role-play area by taping a disc of card to a piece of dowelling, then decorating it with woollen hair, a face, and fabric or paper clothing. Help the children to solve practical problems such as 'How big?', 'How long?' and 'How many?'.

KUW Encourage the children to select tools to cut and join materials while making their puppets to inspire mathematical language such as 'longer', 'shorter', 'bigger' and 'smaller'.

Stepping Stone
Use mathematical language in play.

Early Learning Goal
Use developing mathematical ideas and methods to solve practical problems.

Group size
Small groups.

What you need
A selection of toys (some commercial, others made by the children); two tables; chairs; toy till; real or play money; calculator; labels; strips of paper; notepads; pens; wrapping paper; paper bags; gift boxes.

Home links
Ask parents and carers to encourage their children to use mathematical language at home during play, such as counting pieces in a jigsaw, comparing the size of teddies and estimating the number of beads in a pot.

Creature creation

Stepping Stone
Show curiosity about numbers by offering comments or asking questions.

Early Learning Goal
Use developing mathematical ideas and methods to solve practical problems.

Group size
Small groups.

What you need
Play dough; six small boxes, tubs or baskets, labelled 1 to 6; variety of small objects that can be stuck into play dough, such as buttons, beads, short lengths of plastic straws, card shapes, corks, sequins and so on; dice numbered 1 to 6; a sheet of A5 paper for each child.

Preparation
Place the small objects into the six labelled containers.

What to do

■ Provide each child with a lump of play dough to manipulate into the shape of an imaginary creature.

■ Explain to the children that they are going to play a game to collect small objects that they can use as crazy features for their creatures, for example, card wings, straw ears, sequin eyes and so on.

■ Place the six labelled containers on the table and ask each child to sit their play-dough creature on a sheet of paper in front of them.

■ Choose a child to throw the dice. If 4 is shown, for example, they must select one object from container number 4. It can then be pressed into the play-dough creature to create one crazy feature.

■ The dice is then passed on to the next player.

■ Play continues until all the children have six crazy features on their creatures.

■ Encourage the children to keep count of how many features are on their creatures.

■ Ask questions such as, 'What number do you need to collect a crazy eye?', 'How many more features do you need to finish your creature?' and so on.

■ Invite younger children to play the game in pairs with an adult helper.

■ Provide older children with two dice to reinforce addition and subtraction skills.

More ideas

■ Pose practical problems such as, 'How many cups do we need to make sure that no one is left out?'.

■ Use small-world animals to ask questions such as, 'How many pairs of legs does one dog have?', 'What about two dogs?' and so on.

Other curriculum areas

PD During team games, invite the children to work out how many beanbags, hoops or balls are needed for each team to make the game fair.

PSED After cooking, encourage the children to share out the products so that everyone has, for example, two each, or so that two are saved for absent children.

Mathematical development

Buying cakes

What to do

■ Sing the rhyme 'Five Currant Buns' with the children.

■ Invite the children to cut and stick a picture of a cake or bun on to each of the 12 sheets of card.

■ Help the children to label each picture with a price between 1p and 3p.

■ Ask the children to draw one to six spots on the reverse side of each picture to create 12 cards for a game.

■ Provide two to four players with ten one-penny coins each.

■ Lay the game cards, spot-side showing, in front of the children and place a small, empty pot near by.

■ Choose a child to throw the dice. If, for example, a 2 is shown, one game card with two spots should be collected.

■ The player should then read out the price of the cake on the other side of the card, and count the correct number of one-penny coins to put in the pot.

■ The game card should be retained and the dice can then be passed on to the next player.

■ Repeat the process until there are no more game cards left.

■ The winner is the player who has bought the most cakes.

■ Help younger children to price all the cakes at 1p.

■ Ask older children to write the numerals 1 to 6 on the reverse side of the game cards.

More ideas

■ Challenge the children with questions such as, 'Should a player miss a turn if they only have 2p left and the cake on the game card costs 3p?'.

■ Ask the children questions such as, 'Do you think that a player should have another turn if they throw a 5 on the dice and there are no game cards left showing five spots?'.

Other curriculum areas

CD Invite the children to use available resources to create props to support role-play about the rhyme 'Five Currant Buns'.

PSED Involve the children in agreeing to simple rules for the number game and encourage them to take responsibility in their implementation.

Stepping Stone
Show confidence with numbers by initiating or requesting number activities.

Early Learning Goal
Use developing mathematical ideas and methods to solve practical problems.

■

Group size
Two to four children.

■

What you need
Pictures of cakes or buns; 12 sheets of A5 card; pens; ten real or play one-penny coins for each player; small pot; 12 white sticky labels; dice; copy or knowledge of the rhyme 'Five Currant Buns' (Traditional).

Home links
Encourage parents and carers to play number or dice games at home with their children.

Mathematical development

Six snug teddy bears

Early Learning Goal
Use developing mathematical ideas and methods to solve practical problems.

Group size
Six children.

What you need
Three A4 card copies of the photocopiable sheet 'Snug teddies' on page 85, cut into six pictures; six labels showing the numbers 1 to 6 (approximately 4cm x 4cm); coloured pencils; six rectangles of colourful felt or another none-fraying fabric (approximately 15cm x 20cm), including three blue; wide variety of small, colourful felt shapes; display area at the children's height; staple gun or drawing pins (adult use).

Home links
Send home a copy of the rhyme.

What to do
■ Say the following rhyme with the children:

Six snug teddy bears, closing their eyes, one got up, and then there were five.
Five snug teddy bears, loudly snore, one got up, and then there were four.
Four snug teddy bears, having a dream, one got up, and then there were three.
Three snug teddy bears, wrapped in blue, one got up, and then there were two.
Two snug teddy bears, having some fun, one got up, and then there was one.
One snug teddy bear, wanted his mum, he got up, and then there were none.

■ Provide each child with a rectangle of felt to fold and glue to create a pocket (see diagram). 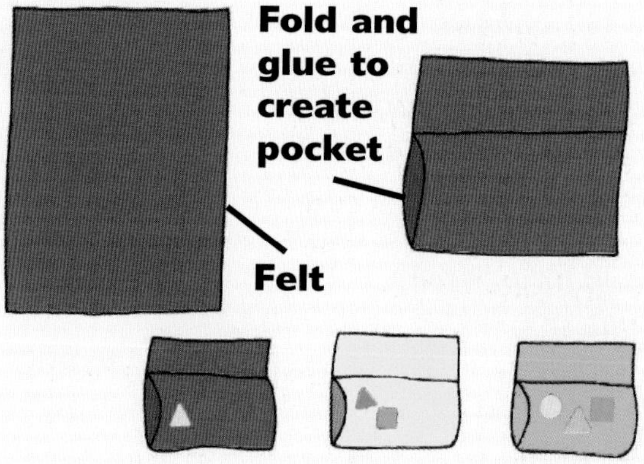
■ Invite the children to glue one felt shape on to the first pocket, two on the second, and so on up to six on the sixth pocket. Make sure that pockets 4, 5 and 6 are blue.

Fold and glue to create pocket

Felt

■ Next, provide each child with a teddy-bear picture to colour in. Label the finished pictures 1 to 6 and place them in the appropriate pockets.
■ Staple or pin the pockets in numerical order to create an interactive number line.
■ When the children are not looking, change the position of one or more teddies. Do the children notice the error? Repeat using a different teddy.
■ For younger children, begin with three pockets.
■ Encourage older children to sew the pockets.

Other curriculum areas
CLL — Help the children to write number words on the nightcaps. Can they still spot the errors?
PD — Help the children to devise actions to accompany the rhyme.

More ideas
■ Occasionally rearrange the order of the teddies during the day or the following week, for the children to correct.
■ Create up to ten pockets.

Mathematical development

In this chapter, the activities focus on the cluster 'Calculating'. The children will be challenged to use vocabulary involved in adding and subtracting, to use language such as 'more' or 'less', and to find 'one more' or 'one less' than a number from one to ten.

Trip, trap

What to do

■ Read the story 'The Three Billy Goats Gruff' to the children.
■ Draw the outline of a river and a bridge on to a sheet of A1 paper and invite the children to paint the scene (see illustration).

■ Ask a child to paint a troll's face on to a small disc of card to place under the bridge.
■ Provide each child with a card copy of the photocopiable sheet. Invite them to colour in the goat and help them to cut around the outline.
■ Use Blu-Tack to secure the three goats on to the left-hand side of the bridge.

■ Display the scene at the children's height and ask them, 'How many goats are in the picture?'.
■ Retell the story and as you do, move the goats, one at a time, across the bridge. Ask questions such as, 'How many goats are in the picture now?', 'How many goats will be in the picture if one goat is in the field and two goats are on the bridge?' and so on.
■ Invite younger children to point or touch the goats as they count.
■ Encourage older children to reposition the goats as the story is retold.

More ideas

■ Remove one goat at a time and talk with the children about 'taking away' and 'subtraction'.
■ Introduce a fourth goat to inspire vocabulary involved in adding and subtracting up to 4.

Other curriculum areas

PD Count children as they slither, roll, crawl, jump and so on across a soft mat and a low bench representing a river and a bridge.

CLL Retell the story and encourage the children to anticipate how many goats will be on the bridge and in the fields.

Goals for the Foundation Stage

Stepping Stone
Separate a group of three or four objects in different ways, beginning to recognise that the total is still the same.

Early Learning Goal
In practical activities and discussion begin to use the vocabulary involved in adding and subtracting.

■

Group size
Three children for the making of the picture; any size for the discussion.

■

What you need
A copy of the story 'The Three Billy Goats Gruff' (Traditional); large sheet of A1 paper; paints; painting equipment; small disc of card; three card copies of the photocopiable sheet 'Billy goat' on page 86; coloured pencils; Blu-Tack; display area at the children's height.

Home links
Ask parents and carers to encourage their children to separate and count a group of three objects during everyday activities at home, for example, toys while playing or ingredients when cooking.

Seven dwarfs

Early Learning Goal
In practical activities and discussion begin to use the vocabulary involved in adding and subtracting.

Group size
Small groups.

What you need
A pictorial story-book of 'Snow White and the Seven Dwarfs' (Ladybird Books); seven cardboard tubes; seven rectangles of fabric (large enough to cover the tubes); seven triangles of fabric (large enough to flop over the top of the tube); copy of the photocopiable sheet 'Dwarf faces' on page 87, cut into seven pictures; cotton wool; glue; coloured pencils.

Home links
Ask parents and carers to provide photographs of their children to create a comparative display showing how many children are, for example, four and five years old, have dark and light hair and so on.

What to do
■ Read the story of 'Snow White and the Seven Dwarfs' to the children.
■ Invite the children to create models of the seven dwarfs by gluing the cut-out faces on to seven cardboard tubes, then using rectangles of fabric for cloaks, cotton wool for beards and hair, and triangles of fabric for floppy hats (see diagram).

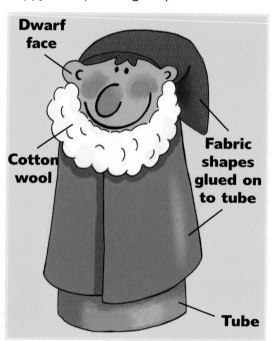

Dwarf face

Cotton wool

Fabric shapes glued on to tube

Tube

■ When the models are complete, use them to play counting games by pretending that they are going to work one, two or three at a time. For example, place the models in a line and ask the children to count how many there are.
■ Remove one of the models and ask the children to count how many are left.
■ Repeat this process until all the models have been removed. Use a variety of mathematical terms to describe subtraction, for example, 'take away', 'minus' and 'one less'.
■ Return the models, one, two or three at a time, and ask the children to count how many there are each time. Use mathematical terms to describe addition, for example, 'one more', 'add one' and 'one extra'.
■ Help younger children to add and subtract one dwarf at a time.
■ Encourage older children to create groups of up to ten everyday objects to count and compare.

More ideas
■ Divide the models, or other objects, into two groups and ask the children to identify the group containing the most models.
■ Use an even number of models to divide into groups, and ask the children to say when the numbers in each group are the same.

Other curriculum areas
CLL   Encourage the children to count and compare the numbers of different characters that they can see in picture books.
KUW   Help the children to count and compare how many boys, girls, adults and pets are in their families or in your setting.

Jump and bump

What to do
■ Provide each child in the group with a card copy of the photocopiable sheet to colour in and cut out around the outline.

■ Help each child to tape a short length of elastic on to the top of their teddy picture.

■ Lay a doll's blanket and pillow on the floor or a table to represent a teddy's bed.

■ Encourage the children to bounce their teddies up and down on the bed as they say the following rhyme:

Five little teddies jumping on the bed, one fell off and bumped his head. Mummy rang the doctor and the doctor said, "No more teddies jumping on the bed."
Four little teddies jumping on the bed,...
and so on until there are no teddies left.

■ After each verse, encourage one child to jump their teddy off the bed, and ask questions such as, 'How many teddies are on the bed?' and 'How many teddies have jumped off the bed at the end of this verse?'.

■ Help younger children during the cutting stage.

■ Invite older children to make two teddies, one for each hand, and to say an adapted version of the rhyme: 'Ten little teddies jumping on the bed, two fell off and bumped their heads', the second verse beginning with 'Eight little teddies' and so on.

More ideas
■ Produce ten to 20 copies of the teddy and invite the children to colour them in matching pairs, for example, two blue, two green and so on. Use the teddies for games such as 'Snap!' and 'Pairs'.

■ Label five or more teddies with numerals and hide them around the room for the children to find. Ask questions such as, 'How many teddies have been found?', 'Which numbers are missing?' and so on.

Other curriculum areas
CD   Help the children to make simple soft-toy teddies to count and compare.

PSED   Invite the children to bring teddy bears from home to share during practical activities based on addition and subtraction.

Come aboard!

What to do
■ Read the story of Noah's ark to the children.

■ Position the toy animals next to the ark and ask questions such as, 'How many animals are there?', 'How many animals are in the ark?', 'How many pairs of animals are there?' and so on.

■ Place two small-world people in the ark to represent Mr and Mrs Noah giving instructions or posing problems for the children to solve. For example, they could say, 'We need three more animals on board', 'If four animals got off the ark, how many would be left on-board?', 'Are there three pairs of animals on-board?' and so on.

■ Encourage younger children to count the animals on and off the ark in ones or twos.

■ Provide older children with up to ten pairs of animals to sort and count.

Other curriculum areas
PD Ask the children to form groups of two, three or four during movement sessions.

CLL Encourage the children to join in singing the song 'The Animals Went in Two by Two' (Traditional).

Home links
Ask parents and carers to encourage their children to play games that involve pairing up pictures or numbers, such as 'Dominoes', 'Happy families' and 'Snap!'.

More ideas
■ Hide some of the animals and ask the children how many are missing.

■ Add extra animals for the children to discover and count.

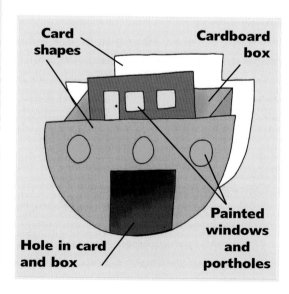

Card shapes

Cardboard box

Hole in card and box

Painted windows and portholes

Mathematical development

Floating bottles

What to do

■ Provide the children with a marker pen to write the numbers 2 to 7 on to six labels and to stick the labels on to the plastic bottles.

■ Place the labelled bottles in a tray of water and provide a fishing net for the children to share.

■ Invite the first child to throw the dice. Ask them to say the number, then to use the fishing net to catch the bottle labelled with the number that is one more. For example, if a 2 is shown, the bottle labelled number 3 should be retrieved.

■ If a player cannot find a bottle with a number that is one more than the number on the dice, play passes to the next child.

■ The game ends when all the bottles have been collected. The winner is the child with the most bottles.

■ Invite younger children to play for fun, rather than for a winner, by letting them have another go, instead of missing a turn, if the bottle that they need is not in the water.

■ Encourage older children to add the numbers on the bottles collected by each player. The winner is the child with the highest score.

More ideas

■ Encourage the children to label the bottles 3 to 9 and to find the bottle that is two more than the number on the dice.

■ Help the children to line up ten green plastic bottles labelled 1 to 10, then to knock them over, one at a time, as they sing the words to the song 'Ten Green Bottles' (Traditional).

Early Learning Goal
In practical activities and discussion begin to use the vocabulary involved in adding and subtracting.
■

Group size
Two children.
■

What you need
Six plastic bottles with lids; water tray; child's fishing net; marker pen; white sticky labels; dice numbered 1 to 6.

Home links
Encourage parents and carers to use the term 'one more' during everyday conversations and practical activities with their children, for example, one more apple in the bowl makes five altogether.

Other curriculum areas

PD Use numbered bottles as skittles to encourage throwing and aiming games. Help the children to keep a running score using a whiteboard or blackboard.

CLL Help the children to label the bottles with number words to encourage word recognition skills.

Mathematical development

Dangling fish

Stepping Stone
Compare two groups of objects, saying when they have the same number.

Early Learning Goal
Use language such as 'more' or 'less' to compare two numbers.

Group size
Small groups.

What you need
Two sheets of blue A1 card; a fish-shaped template for each child (approximately A5 size); A5 paper in four different colours; string; sticky tape; paper clips; lengths of blue wool (between 5cm and 30cm); display area at the children's height.

Preparation
Invite the children to help you to cut the blue card to create two shapes representing fish bowls. Secure the shapes side by side on a display board. Attach a length of string across the top of each shape.

What to do

■ Provide each child with two or three sheets of coloured paper and a fish template. Support them as they draw around it, cut out the shapes and tape a length of blue wool on to each shape.

■ Help the children to put a paper clip on to the loose end of each length of wool. Use the paper clips to hang the paper fish along the string attached to the top of both fish bowls – for example, three fish in the first bowl and four fish in the second (see diagram).

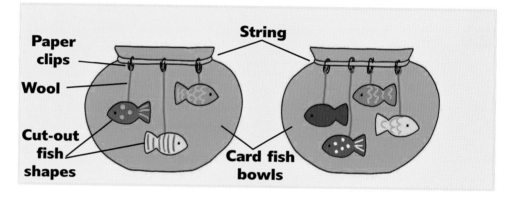

■ Ask the children questions such as, 'Are there more fish in the first bowl?', 'Do the bowls have the same number of fish?' and so on.

■ Repeat the activity by hanging a different number of fish in each bowl.

■ For younger children, hang between one and five fish in each bowl.

■ Ask older children more detailed questions such as, 'Which bowl has the most red fish?'.

More ideas

■ Encourage the children to make fish of different sizes so that they can count a group of big fish, for example, and compare the number with a group of small fish.

■ Help the children to create counting mobiles by hanging groups of two or more paper fish from dowelling or covered coat-hangers.

Home links
Suggest to parents and carers that they buy their children a counting frieze to display at home and to use it with them to encourage an awareness of words such as 'more', 'less' and 'the same as'.

Other curriculum areas

CLL   Invite the children to decorate groups of paper fish with different patterns such as stripes, spots and crosses to encourage descriptive language while counting.

CD   Help the children to use paint or collage materials to create a counting big book showing imaginary underwater creatures.

Mathematical development

Hidden jewels

What to do
■ While the children are not looking, hide five to ten jewels in the sand, then encourage the children to find them.
■ As each jewel is found, invite the children to place them in a row on the surface of the sand. Introduce the words 'one more' in a variety of different ways, for example, 'That makes one more red jewel', 'How many jewels will we have if we find one more?' and so on.

■ Repeat the activity but this time provide each child with a small container to collect the jewels.
■ When all the jewels have been found, ask questions such as, 'Who has found more than two red jewels?', 'Has anyone found less than three yellow jewels?', 'Have you found more red or blue jewels?' and so on.
■ Invite younger children to work together in pairs to share the counting tasks.
■ For older children, hide up to 20 jewels in the sand for them to find, compare and count.

More ideas
■ Provide the children with a clipboard and pens to match the colour of the jewels hidden in the sand. Invite them to keep a tally on their clipboard by drawing one spot to match the colour of each jewel found.
■ Ask the children to compare the number of jewels in their container with their tally count by asking questions such as, 'How many red jewels are in your container?', 'Are there more, less or the same number of red spots on your clipboard?' and so on.

Other curriculum areas
CD Encourage the children to count and compare as they decorate crowns, made out of card, using a row of shiny paper shapes to represent colourful jewels.

PSED Decorate biscuits, either commercial or made by the children, using icing and coloured sweets. Use the experience to inspire terms such as 'more than', 'less than' and 'sharing'. Check for any food allergies and dietary requirements.

Stepping Stone
Say with confidence the number that is one more than a given number.

Early Learning Goal
Use language such as 'more' or 'less' to compare two numbers.
■
Group size
Small groups.
■
What you need
A sand tray containing dry sand; five to ten colourful objects to represent jewels, for example, large beads, old jewellery and large buttons; a small container for each child.

Home links
Ask parents and carers for unwanted objects that could be used as jewels or treasure.

Four-eyed monster

Stepping Stone
Separate a group of three or four objects in different ways, beginning to recognise that the total is still the same.

Early Learning Goal
Use language such as 'more' or 'less' to compare two numbers.

Group size
Small groups.

What you need
A cardboard box for each child; paints; painting equipment; cut-out card shapes; Blu-Tack.

What to do
■ Provide each child with a cardboard box and some colourful paints.
■ Encourage the children to use their creative imagination to turn their boxes into monsters. Explain that they do not need to include eyes as these will be put on later.
■ When the monster models are complete, provide each child with four card shapes, for example, four triangles or four ovals, and explain that these shapes are going to be the eyes for their monster.

■ Help the children to draw a dark spot in each eye to create a pupil and to place a small ball of Blu-Tack on the reverse side.
■ Ask each child to position the four eyes on their model and to count how many eyes their monster has.
■ Next, ask each child to remove the four eyes on their monster and replace them in another position.
■ Ask the children to recount how many eyes their monster has.
■ Repeat this process several times until the children begin to recognise that the total number of eyes is still the same.
■ Ask younger children to separate a group of three eyes.
■ Invite older children to cut out the shapes for the monster eyes.

More ideas
■ The monster models could have other removable parts to count, for example, arms, ears or legs.
■ Ask the children to move four monsters in different places around the room, to encourage awareness that the total number remains the same.

Home links
Invite the children to take their monsters home and to talk about them with their parents and carers.

Other curriculum areas
PSED Encourage a group of children to work together to create a shared model of a monster for the activity.

KUW Provide a selection of pictures of animals and help the children to count attributes such as the number of eyes, legs, wings, ears and so on.

Out and about

What to do

■ Take the children on a local walk and talk about the variety of interesting or familiar sights en route, for example, buildings, signs, trees and so on.

■ When back inside, provide the children with nine sheets of A5 card and invite them to draw nine of the sights that they observed during the walk.

■ Help the children to stick the nine pictures on to the grid using Blu-Tack, and to join in a game.

■ The players should take turns to throw both dice. If a letter 'a' and a number 2 are shown, for example, the picture in space 'a2' on the grid should be removed.

■ If the picture in the space on the grid has already been removed, play passes on to the next child.

■ Continue until the grid is empty. The player who has collected the most pictures is the winner.

■ Invite younger children to play in pairs or in small teams.

■ Ask older children questions such as, 'How many pictures are left on the grid?', 'Are there more pictures in row "a" or in row "b"?' and so on.

More ideas

■ Invite the children to use the collection of pictures to help them to recall the walk.

■ Ask the children questions such as, 'What did you see first?', 'What did you see after the church?' and so on.

Home links
Invite parents and carers to join the walk to have extra adult assistance and to share their knowledge of the area or points of local interest.

Other curriculum areas

PSED Help the children to co-operate in pairs to play the game 'Battleships'.

KUW Show the children an Ordnance Survey map and point out the grid lines and some of the landmark signs and symbols.

Ten fat sausages

Stepping Stone
Find the total number of items in two groups by counting all of them.

Early Learning Goal
Use language such as 'more' or 'less' to compare two numbers.

■

Group size
Any size.

■

What you need
A copy or knowledge of the rhyme 'Ten Fat Sausages' (Traditional); Plasticine; two toy frying pans (or similar); two trays; room with enough space to run safely; music tapes or CDs; tape recorder or CD player.

Home links
Encourage parents and carers to involve their children in counting and comparing items at home, saying, for example, 'I have three fishfingers, you have two, you have one less than me'.

What to do

■ Sing the rhyme 'Ten Fat Sausages' with the children.
■ Invite each child to roll one or more sausage shapes using a small lump of Plasticine.
■ Divide the children into two teams (with an equal number in each team). Ask all the children in each team to place their sausages on a tray.
■ Each team should then form a line a few metres away from their tray of sausages.
■ Provide the first child in each team with a toy frying pan.

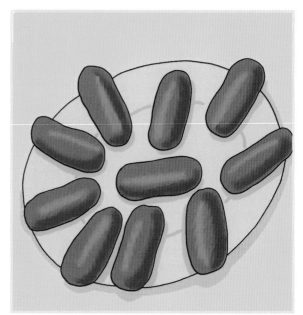

■ Start playing some music. Invite each of the two children holding the frying pans to run up to their team's tray of sausages and place one sausage in their pan. They should then run back to their team to hand over the frying pan to the next player.
■ The second player in each team should take the frying pan and return to the tray to collect a second sausage.
■ Play continues until the music stops.
■ Encourage the children to count the total number of sausages in each frying pan. The team with the most sausages is the winner.
■ Encourage younger children to remove the sausages from the pan, one at a time, when they count their total.
■ Invite older children to collect and count the sausages two at a time.

More ideas

■ Play the same game using plastic toy sausages.
■ Provide the first player in each team with a frying pan full of sausages. Ask the players to remove the sausages, one or two at a time, on to the tray. The winner is the team with the least sausages in their pan when the music stops.

Other curriculum areas

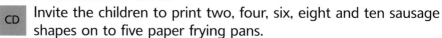

CD   Invite the children to print two, four, six, eight and ten sausage shapes on to five paper frying pans.

PD   Play the game outside using large hoops, tennis rackets and beanbags or balls.

One more instrument

What to do
■ Sit the children in a circle and place the ten instruments on a table or mat in the middle.

■ Encourage the children to choose a favourite song or nursery rhyme that has ten verses, such as 'Ten Green Bottles' or 'There Were Ten in the Bed' (Traditional).

■ Alternatively, choose a song that can be sung with ten made-up verses, such as 'Here We Go Round the Mulberry Bush' (Traditional).

■ Ask a child to select an instrument to play while singing the first verse with the other children.

■ Pause after the first verse and ask questions such as, 'How many instruments were being played?', 'How many instruments are left on the mat?' and so on.

■ Alternatively, pose simple problems, for example, 'If one more child plays an instrument, how many will be playing altogether and how many children will not have an instrument?'.

■ Encourage a second child to select an instrument and invite both children to play the instruments during the second verse. Then ask the children similar questions or pose similar problems for them to solve.

■ Invite a third child to select an instrument to play during the third verse, and so on until all the children have an instrument to play and none are left on the mat.

■ Help younger children to choose a song with five verses.

■ Provide older children with a recurring number problem to solve by asking 'How many children will have to share an instrument if one is removed?'.

More ideas
■ Label the instruments 1 to 5, or 1 to 10, for the children to collect and play in numerical order.

■ Write ten number cards, each showing the addition of one, for example, 0+1, 1+1, 2+1 and so on. Invite one child at a time to turn over a card, work out the sum, then select the instrument with the matching number label.

Other curriculum areas
CD Encourage the children to paint a number frieze based on a favourite counting rhyme.

PSED Use the main activity to promote turn-taking, patience and co-operation between groups of children.

Stepping Stone
Show an interest in number problems.

Early Learning Goal
Find one more or one less than a number from one to 10.
■
Group size
Up to ten children.
■
What you need
Ten percussion instruments.

Home links
Ask parents and carers if they have a favourite counting rhyme from the past or from a different country that they could teach the group of children.

Make a snake

Early Learning Goal
Find one more or one less than a number from one to 10.

Group size
Small groups.

What you need
Ten rectangles of card (approximately 5cm x 6cm); small magnet; string; dowelling rod (or old pencil); ten metal paper clips; ten small sticky labels; coloured felt-tipped pens.

Preparation
Create a 'magnetic fishing rod' by tying the string to the dowelling rod, then tying or taping the magnet to the end of the string. Use two of the rectangles of card to draw the outline of a snake's head and a snake's tail.

Home links
Help individual children to make their own snake game to take home.

What to do
■ Provide the children with the ten rectangles of card to decorate to represent sections of a colourful snake.
■ Help the children to write the numbers 1 to 10 on to ten sticky labels.
■ Ask the children to stick label number 1 on to the snake's head and number 10 on to the snake's tail. The numbers 2 to 9 should then be placed on the remaining eight cards.
■ Invite the children to place a paper clip on to each decorated card.
■ Ask the children to scatter the cards with the numbers showing. Then invite a child to pick up one of the cards using the magnetic fishing rod and to place it in front of them.
■ The second player must use the rod to pick up a card that shows a number 'one more' or 'one less' than the number on the first card. For example, if the first card was number 6, the next card to find should be 5 or 7. The second card must be placed in the correct position next to the first card and the fishing rod passed on to the next player.
■ This process is repeated until all ten cards are in numerical order and the snake is complete.
■ Ask younger children to create a snake showing numbers 1 to 5.
■ Encourage older children to make a snake using 15 to 20 sections.

More ideas
■ Make a curved or curly snake.
■ Place the numbers face down to make a game of chance.

Other curriculum areas
CLL Invite the children to write the number words on to the snake sections to encourage reading skills.
CD Provide finger-paints, collage materials or paper shapes to decorate the game.

Mathematical development

The building site

What to do
■ Place an assortment of toy diggers and trucks on to a sheet of brown paper or fabric to represent a muddy building site.
■ Provide each child with ten bricks to place in a row and a builder's helmet to wear.
■ Ask the children to count how many bricks they have.
■ Next, manoeuvre one of the trucks or diggers around the 'building site' to collect one brick from each child.

■ Ask the children to count how many bricks they have left. Say together, 'Nine is one less than ten' or 'Ten take away one is nine'.
■ Repeat this process until all the bricks have been removed.
■ Next, use the toy truck or digger to return one brick at a time to each child. Use the terms 'add' and 'one more', for example, 'Six is one more than five' or 'Five add one is six'.
■ Repeat this process until all the bricks have been returned.
■ Provide younger children with five bricks.
■ For older children, remove and return two or more bricks at a time.

More ideas
■ Play the same game in the sand tray or outside in a real patch of mud.
■ Organise other play situations to reinforce the same mathematical terms, for example, toy farm animals moving in and out of a field, play people leaving and returning to a house or soft toys 'jumping' in and out of a basket.

Other curriculum areas
PD Invite the children to pretend to be diggers or trucks while they move and count large, soft play equipment around an imaginary building site to create an obstacle course to use.
CD Help the children to paint or make a collage of ten boxes to represent colourful bricks for an interactive counting display based on building a new wall for Humpty Dumpty.

Stepping Stone
Say with confidence the number that is one more than a given number.

Early Learning Goal
Find one more or one less than a number from one to 10.
■
Group size
Small groups.
■
What you need
Small building bricks; toy diggers and dumper trucks; a toy builder's helmet for each child (optional); large sheet of brown paper or fabric.

Home links
Encourage parents and carers to use the words 'one more' and 'one less' during their everyday activities with their children.

Round the garden

Stepping Stone
Find the total number of items in two groups by counting all of them.

Early Learning Goal
Find one more or one less than a number from one to 10.

Group size
Small groups or individual children.

What you need
A copy of the photocopiable sheet 'Moving bears' on page 89; coloured pens or pencils; a teddy bear for each child.

Home links
Invite the children to bring in their favourite teddies and place them in two large boxes or baskets. Ask them to find the total number of teddies by counting them in both boxes.

What to do
■ Say the rhyme 'Round and Round the Garden' with the children, then encourage them to adapt the rhyme by changing the last few words, for example, 'Round and round the garden like a teddy bear, one step, two steps, dancing everywhere', or 'clapping in the air', 'hopping here and there', 'jumping up the stair', 'sitting in a chair' and so on.

■ Provide each child with a teddy bear to make dance, clap, hop, jump, sit and so on as they say the adapted rhymes.
■ Next, give each child coloured pens or pencils and a copy of the photocopiable sheet, and invite them to colour in the bears.
■ When the sheets are complete, use them to encourage sorting and counting skills by asking the children questions such as, 'How many teddies are clapping?', 'How many teddies are sitting?', 'How many teddies are hopping?', 'How many teddies are there altogether?', 'How many red teddies are there?' and so on.
■ Provide younger children with an enlarged photocopiable sheet to share during a group activity.
■ For older children, adapt the photocopiable sheet by writing colour words in a chart and the initial letters on the teddies, for example, r = red, b = blue and so on.

More ideas
■ Divide unusual or interesting objects into two groups and hide them in the room, or in a safe outdoor area, for the children to find and count.
■ Enlarge two copies of the photocopiable sheet to colour in and cut out for matching, sorting and counting games such as 'Pairs' and 'Snap!'.

Other curriculum areas
CD Provide clay or salt dough for the children to model teddy-bear shapes. Invite them to paint the models, then use them for an interactive counting display.

PSED Organise a teddy bears' picnic using real or play food, and encourage the children to share out and count the food items on to plates, for example, one apple and two biscuits, or three strawberries and one cake.

Mathematical development

Tea for two

What to do

■ Read or tell the story 'Goldilocks and the Three Bears' to the children.

■ Set up the role-play area to represent Goldilocks' house, including a low table, two chairs and the ten play utensils.

■ Provide the children with a doll to represent Goldilocks and a toy bear to represent Baby Bear.

■ Invite the children to imagine that Goldilocks has invited Baby Bear around for tea to say 'sorry' for eating all his porridge and breaking his favourite chair.

■ Encourage the children to seat the two toys at the table and to share the ten play utensils equally between Goldilocks and Baby Bear.

■ Use the activity to encourage sorting and matching skills by asking the children to compare the two place settings, saying when they have the same number of utensils.

■ Ask the children questions such as, 'How many items does Baby Bear have on the table?', 'Do you think that Goldilocks has more, less or the same number of items compared to Baby Bear?', 'If you give Baby Bear an extra spoon, will he have more or less spoons than Goldilocks?' and so on.

■ Provide younger children with just six play utensils to share between the two toys.

■ Give older children extra play utensils to share equally between the two toys.

More ideas

■ Ask the children to look away while you remove one or more of the utensils. Can they work out what, or how many, items are missing?

■ Instead of sharing utensils, invite the children to share items of food (real, wrapped food or play food) between the two toys.

Other curriculum areas

PSED Encourage a group of children to share real utensils during a cooking activity.

PD Organise some team games for the children and encourage them to share resources such as balls and hoops equally.

Pizza shapes

Early Learning Goal
Begin to relate addition to combining two groups of objects and subtraction to 'taking away'.

■

Group size
Small groups.

■

What you need
Discs of buff-coloured paper or card (approximately 25cm in diameter); variety of coloured paper shapes to represent slices of food (yellow triangles for cheese, pink squares for ham, red discs for tomatoes, brown discs for sausage, green ovals for olives, yellow rectangles for pineapple and so on); red pencils; glue; checked drape or old table-cloth; display board at the children's height.

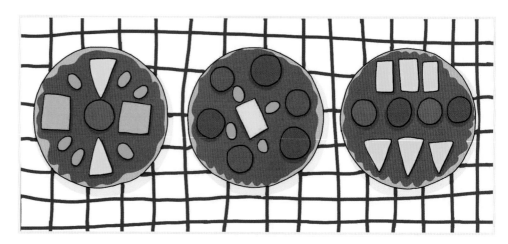

What to do

■ Provide each child with a disc of buff-coloured paper to represent a pizza base and invite them to colour it in using red pencils to represent a layer of tomato sauce.

■ Encourage the children to decorate their pizzas using a total of ten to 12 shapes. Ask each child to select shapes that represent two different food types, for example, cheese and ham, or sausage and tomato.

■ Ask the children questions to develop an awareness of addition, for example, 'There are five cheese shapes and four ham shapes on your pizza, so how many shapes are there altogether?'.

■ Encourage the children to develop an awareness of 'taking away' by asking them to count how many shapes are left on their pizzas after one or more have been removed.

■ Finally, invite the children to glue the shapes on to their pizza bases. When the pizzas are dry, mount them on a display board covered with a checked drape or an old table-cloth to represent a pizza party feast.

■ Provide younger children with a total of five to eight shapes to add and take away.

■ Give older children a total of 15 or 20 shapes.

More ideas

■ Encourage the children to make repeated patterns on their pizzas.

■ Use the display with the children to inspire addition, for example, 'How many pizzas have slices of cheese?', 'How many pizzas have sausage and ham?' and so on.

Other curriculum areas

KUW — Create a simple pictorial graph showing the children's favourite foods to count and compare.

CLL — Encourage the children to join in singing the song 'Ten Fat Sausages' (Traditional).

Balls and boxes

What to do

◼ Show the children how to secure three to six containers in a cluster on to cardboard using masking tape to hold them firmly in position. Cut away the excess cardboard around the base of the containers.

◼ Invite the children to decorate the sides of the containers and the base using colourful paints. When the model is dry, help them to varnish it with PVA glue. Leave it to dry.

◼ Provide the children with six sheets of coloured paper to scrunch up into six tight balls. Invite them to drop the balls into the containers, a little distance away from them, holding one ball at a time.

◼ Encourage the children to count how many of the six paper balls landed in the containers. Let them play several times.

◼ Use the activity to inspire adding and subtracting by asking the children questions such as, 'How many balls have you dropped?', 'How many balls have you got left?' and so on.

◼ Encourage the children to solve simple problems by asking questions such as, 'If you have six balls and you drop two, how many balls will you have left?'.

◼ Invite younger children to make three paper balls to drop and count.

◼ Make the game more challenging for older children by placing score labels on the sides of the boxes. Encourage them to add up their total score after they have dropped all six balls into the containers.

More ideas

◼ Invite the children to aim and throw the balls into the containers instead of dropping them.

◼ Encourage the children to play the game with a friend and to write down the number of balls that they manage to get into the containers each turn.

Stepping Stone
Use own methods to solve a problem.

Early Learning Goal
Begin to relate addition to combining two groups of objects and subtraction to 'taking away'.

◼

Group size
Small groups.

◼

What you need
Three to six boxes or tubs in different sizes; masking tape; coloured paper; paints; painting equipment; cardboard; heavy-duty scissors (adult use); PVA glue.

Home links
Encourage parents and carers to come to your setting to play the 'box and ball' game with their children.

Other curriculum areas

PD Play a similar game outside with the children using large soft balls and large cardboard boxes or crates pushed together into a close cluster.

PSED Encourage the children to play other games that involve turn-taking, counting and sharing equipment, for example, child-made or commercial board games such as 'Snakes and ladders', and 'Hopscotch'.

Bug in boots

Early Learning Goal
Begin to relate addition to combining two groups of objects and subtraction to 'taking away'.

■

Group size
Small groups.

■

What you need
A display board at the children's height, covered with plain backing paper; ten sheets of A5 card; 11 discs of coloured paper (approximately A4 size); glue; Blu-Tack or Velcro; coloured pens; paints; dice showing dots or numbers 1 to 6.

Home links
Invite the children to take a mini version of the game home to play with their parents or carers.

What to do
■ Help the children to glue 11 discs of coloured paper along a display board. Each disc should slightly overlap the previous one to create a long caterpillar.
■ Encourage the children to paint a caterpillar's face on to the first disc and paint ten short lines on the backing paper to represent ten legs, protruding from the remaining ten discs.
■ Invite the children to draw a colourful picture of a boot on to each of the ten sheets of A5 card.

■ Use Blu-Tack or Velcro to secure the boot pictures on to the ten caterpillar legs along the display board.
■ Provide the children with a dice to share. Ask them to take it in turns to throw the dice and to remove the correct number of boots from the caterpillar.
■ When all the boots have been removed, ask each child to count how many boot pictures they have collected. The child with the most boots is the winner.
■ Alternatively, place the boot pictures in a pile. Ask the children to take it in turns to throw the dice and attach the correct number of boots to the caterpillar. The child who gives the caterpillar his last boot is the winner.
■ Provide younger children with a dice showing one, two and three dots.
■ Invite older children to make a caterpillar that is 15 or more discs long with 15 or more boot pictures.

More ideas
■ Invite the children to use a large sponge cut into the shape of a boot to create ten printed picture cards for the game.
■ Help the children to make number spinners to use instead of a dice.

Other curriculum areas
CD Invite the children to use collage materials or coloured sticky paper to create a mini, table-top version of the same game.

CLL Create an interactive display using a selection of real boots and shoes for the children to talk about as they sort, match, count and pair up.

Fun with frogs!

Stepping Stone
Separate a group of three or four objects in different ways, beginning to recognise that the total is still the same.

Early Learning Goal
Begin to relate addition to combining two groups of objects and subtraction to 'taking away'.
■
Group size
Five children for the making of the pictures; any size for the game.
■
What you need
Five copies of the photocopiable sheet 'Speckled frog' on page 90; coloured pens or pencils; scissors; A4 card; laminator or sticky-backed plastic; safe outdoor area; the rhyme 'Five Little Frogs' from *Apusskidu* chosen by Beatrice Harrop et al (A & C Black).

What to do
■ Sing the rhyme 'Five Little Frogs' with the children.
■ Provide each child with a copy of the photocopiable sheet and ask them to colour it in and cut it out.
■ Help each child to glue their frog picture on to a sheet of card, then laminate it or cover it with sticky-backed plastic.
■ Take the children to a safe outdoor area. Place the five frog pictures together on the ground and ask the children to count how many there are in total.
■ Now hide the frog pictures in separate places for the children to find and count. Ask them if the total number of pictures is still the same.
■ Play again, but this time ask five children to hide one frog picture each for the rest of the group to find and count.
■ Encourage younger children to hide, find and count three frog pictures.
■ For older children, hide the pictures in different combinations, for example, two frogs in one place, two in another place and one in a third place.

More ideas
■ Invite the children to paint pictures of other characters from popular songs or rhymes to hide and find, for example, five little ducks or five little monkeys.
■ Invite the children to hide, find and count soft toys.

Home links
Send home copies of the photocopiable sheet and of the rhyme 'Five Little Frogs' for the children to sing with their parents or carers.

Other curriculum areas
CLL Encourage the children to join in singing the song 'Five Little Frogs' using the frog pictures as a visual resource.
PSED Invite the children to separate and share a group of finger puppets in different ways during role-play.

Five tiny buns

Stepping Stone
Use own methods to solve a problem.

Early Learning Goal
Begin to relate addition to combining two groups of objects and subtraction to 'taking away'.

Group size
Any size.

What you need
A low table; five small play buns or cakes; one-penny coins; copy or knowledge of the rhyme 'Five Currant Buns' (Traditional); two open-top cake boxes or similar.

What to do
◼ Place five play buns on a low table and invite a child to act as shopkeeper by standing behind it. Sit the rest of the group near by so that they can see the table and buns clearly.

◼ Invite the children to help you to adapt the words of the rhyme 'Five Currant Buns', for example, 'Five tiny buns in a baker's shop, small and round with a grape (or nut, strawberry, sweet and so on) on top. Along came (child's name) with a penny one day,

bought a tiny bun and took it right away. Four tiny buns...' and so on.

◼ Pause after the first verse and give a child a penny to 'buy' a bun from the shopkeeper. Ask the children to count how many buns are left on the table and to join in saying, 'Five take away one is four'.

◼ Continue until there are no more buns left on the table.

◼ Next, encourage the children to join in other role-play situations that involve addition and subtraction. For example, give two children a cake box each and invite the 'shopkeeper' to place two of the buns in one box and three in the other. Ask the children to count how many cakes there are altogether and to join in saying 'Two and three is five'. Repeat using different numbers.

◼ Invite younger children to touch each bun as they count.

◼ Encourage older children to solve problems such as, 'If one bun costs 2p and another costs 1p, how much money will the shopkeeper need?'.

More ideas
◼ Reinforce the activity using different role-play situations, for example, choosing cakes in a café or packing buns for a picnic.

◼ Use real, wrapped buns or cakes that the children can eat after the activity. Remember to check for any food allergies and dietary requirements.

Home links
Ask parents and carers to come to your setting to help their children to make real buns or cakes.

Other curriculum areas
KUW Encourage the children to help you to make real buns or cakes to share and count.

CD Help the children to model play food using Plasticine, play dough, salt dough or clay, for use in role-play.

This chapter focuses on the cluster 'Shape, space and measures'. The activities will encourage the children to compare quantities, to talk about, recognise and re-create simple patterns, to describe solids and flat shapes, and to develop problem-solving skills.

Long or short?

What to do
■ Provide each child with two small lumps of air-drying clay (or salt dough) to roll into two 'worm shapes' of different lengths.
■ Encourage the children to compare the lengths of their worm models using mathematical terms such as 'longer', 'shorter', 'longest' and 'shortest'.
■ Now ask the children to compare the lengths of their worm models with their colourful worm pictures. Ask them questions such as, 'Which model is longer than the red worm?', 'Which model is shorter than the blue worm?' and so on.

■ Help the children to cut or stretch their two worm models so that they match the lengths of the worms on their pictures.
■ When the models are dry, encourage the children to paint them to match the pictures. Then use the sheets and models to create an interactive display to inspire sorting and matching.
■ Help younger children when they are rolling the malleable material into two different lengths.
■ Invite older children to colour an A3 copy of the sheet to provide two extra worm pictures to match and compare to four models.

Home links
Provide each child with one of the worm pictures to take home. Ask parents and carers to help their children to find two items in the house or garden that are longer than the worm picture and two items that are shorter.

More ideas
■ Invite the children to select Plasticine or play dough in the correct two colours to create their worm models.
■ Encourage the children to make a third model, then to place their models in order of length, starting with the shortest.

Other curriculum areas
CLL Invite the children to make up names for two or three worm models, for example, 'Tall Tim', 'Short Sally' and 'Middle-sized Mary'.

KUW Go outside to look at real worms with the children, or create a wormery indoors. Talk about the different lengths of the worms from first-hand observations.

Stepping Stone
Order two items by length.

Early Learning Goal
Use language such as 'greater', 'smaller', 'heavier' or 'lighter' to compare quantities.

Group size
Small groups.

What you need
Malleable materials such as salt dough; modelling boards; safe cutting tools; copy of the photocopiable sheet 'Wiggly worms' on page 91 for each child; laminator or sticky-backed plastic.

Preparation
Invite each child to colour in the worm pictures on their photocopiable sheet, using a different colour for each worm. Laminate the sheets or cover them with sticky-backed plastic, then cut them along the solid lines.

Cheese straws

Stepping Stone
Order two or three items by length.

Early Learning Goal
Use language such as 'greater', 'smaller', 'heavier' or 'lighter' to compare quantities.

Group size
Small groups.

What you need
Ingredients: 125g plain flour; ¼ teaspoon salt; 100g grated cheese; 75g butter or margarine; egg; water. Equipment: plastic mixing bowl; spoons; rolling-pins; blunt knife (adult use); baking tray; weighing scales; oven; oven gloves; hand-washing facilities; clean aprons.

Home links
Ask parents and carers to involve their children in weighing ingredients and in comparing utensils by size when cooking.

What to do
■ Pre-heat the oven.
■ Provide each child with a clean apron and make sure that they wash their hands properly. (If they are going to eat the cheese straws, remember to check for any food allergies and dietary requirements.)
■ Involve the children in all stages of preparation.
■ First, sieve the flour and salt into a mixing bowl and rub in the butter.
■ Add the grated cheese, the egg and a few drops of water. Mix to a stiff paste.
■ Roll out the mixture and invite the children to cut the pastry into strips of various lengths.

■ Encourage the children to help you to place the strips on to a baking tray in order of length. Use the activity to inspire mathematical language by asking questions such as, 'Which strip is the longest?', 'Which strip is the shortest?', 'Which is middle-sized?', 'Are any of the strips the same size?' and so on.
■ Set the oven to 180°C/350°F/Gas Mark 4 and cook the cheese straws for eight to ten minutes.
■ Help younger children during the practical stages of mixing and cutting.
■ Encourage older children to help you to weigh the ingredients.

More ideas
■ Create a café or shop in the structured play area and invite the children to display items of play food in length order.
■ Help the children to knead dough prepared from a packet of bread mix into bread rolls of different sizes.

Other curriculum areas
CD Invite the children to splatter light-brown paint on to different lengths of yellow card to create pretend cheese straws for an interactive sorting display.
PD Encourage the children to stretch, curl, roll and spread their bodies into different shapes and to use mathematical language to describe their shapes, for example, 'tall', 'taller', 'small', 'smaller' and so on.

Mathematical development

Shapes galore

What to do

■ Show the children how to set up and use the art package and encourage them to practise creating small spots or random shapes on the screen.

■ Help each child to print an A4 colour copy of their picture.

■ Now invite each child to use the same art package to create a picture of one large spot or one large random shape, and to print an A4 colour copy of it.

■ Cut the prints and mount them on a display board covered with black backing paper to create a vibrant display.

■ Talk with the children about the shapes in the display and ask questions to encourage size language, for example, 'Is the yellow spot bigger than the green spot?', 'Can you find one big shape and one little shape?' and so on.

■ Provide younger children with hand-over-hand support while they use the computer mouse and keyboard.

■ Encourage older children to cut out their shape prints and glue them on to the display board, allowing them a high degree of independence.

More ideas

■ Help the children to create a counting book of computer-drawn shapes using size language to describe the shapes on each page, for example, 'One small shape', 'Two big shapes', 'Three tiny shapes' and so on.

■ Use the shapes to create a colourful mobile. Encourage the children to describe and compare the shapes using size language.

Other curriculum areas

CD Invite the children to paint a page full of spots in different sizes and to cut different-sized discs of card so as to create long spirals. Help the children to glue the spirals on to the spotty background to create an unusual collage. Use the display to inspire size language.

KUW Play the 'Big and little' game: take the children outside and ask them to take turns to name big and little items alternately, for example, 'A big tree', 'A little flower', 'A big house' and so on.

Early Learning Goal
Use language such as 'greater', 'smaller', 'heavier' or 'lighter' to compare quantities.

■

Group size
Small groups.

■

What you need
A computer; any art package; colour printer; A4 paper; display board at the children's height; black backing paper.

Home links
Ask parents and carers to join their children while they are using the computer. Some of them will be able to offer their help, others might enjoy learning new skills with their children.

Animal money boxes

What to do
■ Show the children the animal pictures and encourage them to talk about the different shapes and sizes of the animals using descriptive language such as 'tiny', 'tall', 'long' and so on.

■ Next, show the children the boxes and 3-D items and ask them to imagine what sort of animal could be represented by each shape. For example, an upside-down tub could resemble a tortoise, a square box could represent an elephant, a long tube could be a snake, and so on.

■ Invite each child to use collage materials to decorate a box, tub or tube to represent an animal of their choice. Encourage them to cut out shapes from coloured card, sticky paper or fabric to represent features such as ears, eyes and tail. Ask the children to name and identify the different shapes as they work.

■ When the animals are complete, help each child to cut a slit in the top of their model to create an animal-themed money box.

■ Provide the children with real or play coins to count and put into their money boxes.

■ Invite younger children to make an imaginary animal.

■ Introduce older children to the mathematical names for some 3-D shapes, for example, 'cube', 'cylinder' and 'sphere'.

More ideas
■ Encourage the children to select suitable components to make an imaginary bird or underwater creature.

■ Invite the children to create model dinosaurs, dragons or monsters.

Other curriculum areas

PSED Encourage a group of children to work together to create a giant-sized model using a range of 2-D and 3-D shapes.

CD Help the children to cut the top and base out of a large cardboard box and add ribbon shoulder straps. Invite the children to turn the hollow shape into a fancy-dress horse, or other animal, by taping a cardboard head and fabric tail on to the box.

Mathematical development

Leafy puzzle

What to do
◾ Take the children outside to observe the patterns and shapes of different leaves.
◾ Select pairs of different leaves for the children to sort and match.

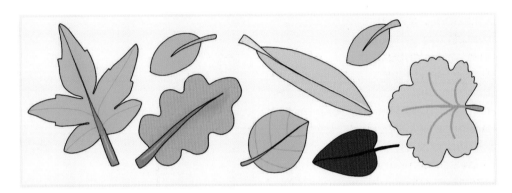

◾ Back inside, provide each child with a copy of the photocopiable sheet.
◾ Encourage the children to identify the five pairs of leaves by observing the matching shapes and patterns.
◾ Invite the children to colour in each pair of leaves so that the leaves in each pair are identical.
◾ Help the children to cut carefully along the solid lines.
◾ Then encourage each child to stick their ten leaf pictures on to ten pieces of card.
◾ Invite the children to use their packs of cards to play matching and sorting games such as 'Snap!' and 'Pairs'.
◾ For younger children, enlarge the photocopiable sheet to make the leaf pictures twice as big. Let a group of children help you to make one set of cards to share during simple matching and sorting activities.
◾ Provide older children with ten pieces of card (approximately 6cm x 10cm) and encourage them to draw and colour in five pairs of matching leaf shapes or flowers to play matching and sorting games.

More ideas
◾ Encourage the children to make repeated patterns using coloured construction bricks.
◾ Look at number patterns in games such as 'Hopscotch' and 'Dominoes'.

Other curriculum areas
CD Help the children to print repeated patterns on fabric using sponge shapes.
CLL Read one of the popular *Elmer* stories by David McKee (Andersen Press). Talk with the children about the shapes and patterns that they can see in the illustrations.

Stepping Stone
Match some shapes by recognising similarities and orientation.

Early Learning Goals
Talk about, recognise and re-create simple patterns.

Group size
Small groups.

What you need
A safe outdoor area where leaves can be collected; the photocopiable sheet 'Matching leaves' on page 92; glue; scissors; card; coloured pens and pencils.

Home links
Invite each child to take a sheet of paper home and ask them to find an interesting pattern to copy and colour in with the help of their parents or carers. Display the patterns in a whole-group big book to inspire observation and discussion.

Model robots

What to do
■ Invite the children to observe and talk about the toy robots.
■ Sketch a large, simple outline of a robot on to a whiteboard or flip chart. Draw a rectangle on the front of the robot picture to represent a control panel.
■ Ask the children to draw shapes such as circles, triangles and squares in the control panel to represent dials, lights, levers and buttons.
■ Help the children to glue and tape several large boxes together to create a 3-D model of a robot. Encourage the children to look at and use the robot sketch as a rough guide during the construction stage.

■ Invite the children to re-create the picture of the control panel using collage materials such as buttons, lids and small boxes to represent the dials and levers. Glue the control-panel collage on to the front of the robot model.
■ When the robot is complete, hang a 'Welcome' sign on it and display it near the entrance to your setting.
■ Ask younger children to use only three or four shapes for the control panel.
■ Invite older children to use five or more shapes for the control panel.

More ideas
■ Encourage the children to paint or print the body, arms and legs of the robot model following a pre-decided pattern, for example, a pattern of circles, an alternating pattern or a repeated pattern.
■ Provide coloured sticky paper shapes, such as circles, oblongs, triangles and squares, for the children to design patterns for the control panel.

Other curriculum areas
CD Glue six rectangles of white or silver paper on to a black background to create the head, body and limbs of a robot. Provide the children with a similar set of paper rectangles to re-create the robot picture.

PSED Encourage a group of children to work together to create a pre-decided model using 3-D materials.

Mathematical development

Patchwork patterns

What to do

▪ Give each child a square template and encourage them to draw around it on to a piece of colourful or patterned fabric. Then help them to cut the fabric to size.

▪ Ask the children to repeat this process until they have a total of 25 squares of fabric between them, cut from the two different fabric samples – for example, 12 red squares and 13 blue squares.

▪ Invite the children to arrange the 25 squares of fabric on to a large piece of plain fabric so that the shapes fit together in a patchwork style.

▪ Challenge the children to talk about, recognise and create simple patterns using the squares of fabric. For example, they could alternate the colours, make random patterns or create repeated patterns.

▪ When the children are happy with their patchwork pattern, help them to glue the squares in place. When the glue is dry, trim the edges of the patchwork pattern to make it look neat. Encourage the children to help you to glue a length of braid around the four edges to create a decorative border.

▪ Sew four loops of wide ribbon along the top edge of the patchwork, then invite the children to thread a length of dowelling through the loops to create a wall hanging.

▪ Help younger children by drawing around the template for them to cut out.

▪ Invite older children to cut out the templates.

More ideas

▪ Provide triangular or oblong templates for the children to draw around and cut out.

▪ Provide colourful wallpaper or wrapping paper for the children to cut to size to decorate work folders or to brighten up old storage boxes.

Other curriculum areas

CD Help the children to cut pieces of fabric to create simple capes, aprons or tabards for their teddies or dolls.

KUW Provide examples or pictures of honeycomb for the children to observe. Help the children to re-create honeycomb patterns using hexagonal templates.

Stepping Stone
Adapt shapes or cut materials to size.

Early Learning Goal
Talk about, recognise and re-create simple patterns.

Group size
Any size.

What you need
A square template for each child (10cm x 10cm); scissors; two different samples of fabric (for example, one red and one blue, or one floral and one stripy), each 40cm x 40cm; large piece of plain fabric (50cm x 50cm); fabric glue; four strips of wide ribbon (10cm long); dowelling (50cm); narrow braid (2m long).

Home links
Encourage the children to look for patterns on walls and furniture at home with their parents or carers.

 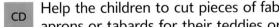

Sand butterflies

Stepping Stone
Show awareness of symmetry.

Early Learning Goal
Talk about, recognise and re-create simple patterns.

Group size
Small groups.

What you need
A sand tray containing dry sand; sheet of coloured card; plastic tray.

Preparation
Cut two squares, two triangles and two circles from the sheet of coloured card, providing two identical sets of three shapes.

What to do
■ Use your finger (or a small stick) to draw a large butterfly outline in the sand. Make sure that the two butterfly wings are the same shape and size on both sides to create a symmetrical image.
■ Ask the children to place one set of card shapes on to one wing of the butterfly. Place the other set of card shapes on to a tray near by.
■ Encourage the children to take it in turns to select a shape from the tray to place on to the empty butterfly wing to create a symmetrical pattern.

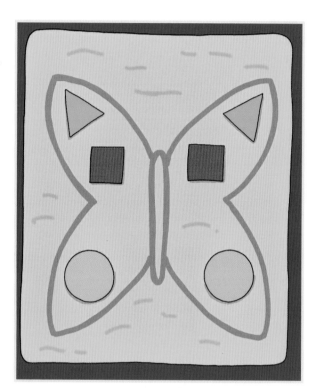

■ Invite the children to repeat the activity several times, placing the shapes in different symmetrical positions each time.
■ Provide younger children with two shapes in each set instead of three.
■ Give older children four or more shapes in each set.

More ideas
■ When the shapes are in the correct position, take a photograph of each sand butterfly. Help the children to mount the photographs in a child-made book or folder containing a collection of symmetrical pictures and patterns.
■ Place a mirror along the centre of the butterfly so that the children can see the symmetrical image of the card shapes in the reflection.
■ Provide the children with a sheet of paper cut into the shape of a symmetrical butterfly. Invite them to paint shapes on to one wing. Fold the butterfly in half to create a symmetrical pattern on the other wing.

Other curriculum areas
KUW Look at photographs or pictures of real butterflies and talk about the symmetrical shapes and colours on their wings.
MD Read the story *The Very Hungry Caterpillar* by Eric Carle (Hamish Hamilton). Encourage the children to describe the picture of the colourful butterfly at the end of the story and ask them if the wings look symmetrical.

Home links
Provide each child with a paper butterfly shape to take home. Ask parents and carers to help their children to draw a simple symmetrical pattern on the wings of the butterfly. Display the butterfly pictures along with several large symmetrical flowers cut from coloured paper, tissue or fabric.

Mathematical development

Circles and spirals

What to do
▪ Help the children to paint large spirals on to discs of black paper. When the paintings are dry, invite the children to glue them on to the display board.
▪ Next, help the children to cut several discs from a variety of collage materials using circular templates as a guide. Talk with them about the shapes, encouraging language such as 'circle', 'round', 'bigger' and 'smaller'.
▪ Invite the children to glue the discs randomly over the spirals on the display board.
▪ Finally, ask the children to colour in and cut out along the thick lines of the spirals on the different-sized photocopiable sheets. Encourage them to compare the sizes and lengths of the spirals using language such as 'longer', 'shorter', 'thinner' and 'wider'.
▪ Help the children to tape the spirals on to the display board so that they dangle freely, creating a triple-layered, abstract picture.
▪ Provide younger children with help when they are gluing and taping their work on to the display board, while still allowing a high degree of independence as they decide where to position each disc and spiral.
▪ Encourage older children to make spheres to hang in the display by scrunching up small sheets of coloured paper.

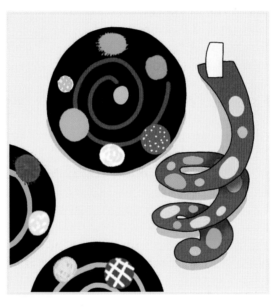

More ideas
▪ Include ovals, crescents and semicircles in the display.
▪ Create a display using rectangles of different shapes and sizes.

Other curriculum areas
CLL Use pictures of abstract paintings by famous artists to inspire discussion about shapes and patterns, for example, *Suprematism* by Kasimir Malevich, or *Composition with Red, Blue and Yellow* by Piet Mondrian.
PD Draw large shapes on the playground. Encourage the children to name or describe the shapes as they hop, skip or jump from one to the other.

Stepping Stone
Use appropriate shapes to make representational models or more elaborate pictures.

Early Learning Goal
Use language such as 'circle' or 'bigger' to describe the shape and size of solids and flat shapes.
▪
Group size
Any size.
▪
What you need
A3, A4 and A5 copies of the photocopiable sheet 'Shapes spiral' on page 93; scissors; colourful collage materials, such as card, fabric and shiny paper; glue; coloured pens; paints; painting equipment; large discs of black paper (20cm to 40cm in diameter); small circular templates (5cm to 15cm in diameter); display board at the children's height, covered with black backing paper.

Home links
Ask the children to look for shapes at home and challenge them to bring in something circular, such as a plastic saucer, or something spherical, such as a sponge ball.

Instrumental shapes

What to do

■ Show the children the percussion instruments and encourage them to explore the different sounds that they make.

■ Help the children to name and identify the different instruments.

■ Challenge the children to find three or more instruments that are round, for example, tambours, cymbals, bells and drums, then to group the instruments into flat shapes (cymbals) and cylinders (drums and tambours).

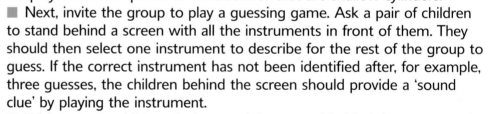

■ Help the children to compare the sizes of the round instruments. For example, drums are deep cylinders compared to tambourines that are shallow cylinders.

■ Next, invite the group to play a guessing game. Ask a pair of children to stand behind a screen with all the instruments in front of them. They should then select one instrument to describe for the rest of the group to guess. If the correct instrument has not been identified after, for example, three guesses, the children behind the screen should provide a 'sound clue' by playing the instrument.

■ With younger children, invite an adult to stand behind the screen and prompt descriptive language.

■ Encourage older children to stand behind the screen one at a time.

More ideas

■ Ask the children to make a pair of mini maracas by taping two lolly-sticks on to two small boxes. Fill each box with dry rice or pasta, then seal it securely using strong tape.

■ Invite the children to make shakers by filling cardboard tubes with small items such as beads, then sealing the ends with discs of coloured paper or fabric.

Other curriculum areas

 Invite the children to make colourful 3-D collages, then to describe and talk about them.

 Play a guessing game that involves describing a selection of everyday items such as toys, food items or utensils.

Mathematical development

Roll to the rhombus!

What to do

■ Place a shape picture in each corner of the room. Help the children to name and identify the shapes.

■ Ask the children to walk quietly around the room, without bumping into one another, listening for you to say either, 'Dance to the diamond!', 'Skip to the square!', 'Tiptoe to the triangle!' or 'Roll to the rhombus!'.

■ When the children hear your instruction, they should dance, skip, tiptoe or roll to the appropriate shape. Emphasise that it is not a race and that they should move carefully, avoiding other children.

■ Repeat the activity by replacing the pictures of 'flat' 2-D shapes with 'solid' 3-D shapes, for example, a cube, sphere, pyramid or cylinder. Help the children to name and identify the shapes and to think of an action to accompany each shape, or use the following examples: 'Crawl to the cube', 'Slide to the sphere', 'Prowl to the pyramid' and 'Sit by the cylinder'.

■ Introduce younger children to the activity by displaying just two shapes in the corners of the room, for example, two diamonds and two triangles.

■ Encourage older children to play the game using two or more 'solid' shapes in each corner.

More ideas

■ Play the game outside if the weather and space are suitable.

■ Invite the children to draw the 2-D shapes or to find the appropriate 3-D shapes for use in the game.

Other curriculum areas

PSED Hide shapes around the room, or in a safe outdoor area, for the children to find and identify.

CLL Place a selection of flat or solid shapes inside a 'feely bag'. Invite each child in turn to touch one shape without seeing it and describe it for the rest of the group to identify.

Stepping Stone
Begin to use mathematical names for 'solid' 3-D shapes and 'flat' 2-D shapes and mathematical terms to describe shapes.

Early Learning Goal
Use language such as 'circle' or 'bigger' to describe the shape and size of solids and flat shapes.

■

Group size
Any size.

■

What you need
A four-cornered room in which the children can move freely and safely; four large pictures of a diamond, square, rhombus and triangle; cube; sphere; pyramid; cylinder.

Home links
Organise an interactive shape display showing a range of pictures and everyday objects that are all the same shape. Ask parents and carers to help their children to contribute one item from home that matches the chosen shape. Change the shape on a regular basis.

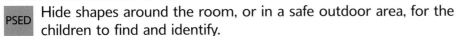

Fish in disguise

Early Learning Goal
Use language such as 'circle' or 'bigger' to describe the shape and size of solids and flat shapes.

Group size
Small groups.

What you need
Water tray; 12 colourful, flat, plastic shapes, such as two large circles, squares and triangles, and two small circles, squares and triangles; a small fishing net or scoop, and a foil or plastic tray for each child; small sticky paper discs; black or blue permanent marker; aprons.

Preparation
Put two small sticky discs on to each plastic shape to represent fish eyes. Use a permanent marker to place a dot in each eye to represent a pupil. Place the shapes in the water tray so that the eyes are looking up, to represent a shoal of colourful imaginary fish.

What to do
■ Provide each child with a fishing net or scoop.
■ Invite the children to take it in turns to 'catch' a particular 'fish' by asking questions such as, 'Can you catch a blue fish?'.
■ When the child has caught the required fish, they should place it on their tray. Then ask questions such as, 'What shape is your blue fish?', 'Is it one of the small shapes or large shapes?' and so on.

Alternatively, ask, 'Can you catch a round fish?'.
■ When the child has selected a round fish, ask questions such as, 'Is your fish bigger or smaller than Amy's round fish?'. Alternatively, pose specific challenges, for example, 'Can you catch a small, square, red fish?'.
■ Either ask the children to throw their 'fish' back after each catch, or let them keep them in their trays. Continue catching until no fish are left in the water.
■ For younger children, keep the shapes simple and help them by reminding them of the shape names.
■ For older children, include some more unusual shapes such as pentagons and hexagons, or use 3-D shapes.

More ideas
■ Invite the children to make 3-D shapes using 2-D shapes, for example, cubes with Polydron rectangles.
■ Help the children to unfold small empty cereal boxes to identify how many 2-D shapes were used. Then invite them to carefully reseal them inside out to obtain blank faces for decorating.

Home links
Ask carers to help their children to collect small boxes for activities about 2-D and 3-D shapes in your setting.

Other curriculum areas
KUW Talk with the children about shapes seen in multicultural patterns such as rangoli patterns.
PD Invite the children to help you to set up an obstacle course using 2-D and 3-D PE equipment, for example, hoops, blocks, boxes, tunnels and mats. Talk about the shapes and sizes of the resources as they are arranged and used.

I spy

What to do

◼ Take the children on a short walk and ask them to look out for different features, such as houses, shops, roads, paths and so on. Alternatively, talk with them about the things that they see on their way to your setting.

◼ Back inside, encourage the children to make a simple floor map for small-world toys. Let them glue several strips of paper on to the card square to represent roads and paths, shiny shapes to create ponds and rivers, and small boxes decorated with windows and doors to create houses, schools and shops.

◼ Next, provide the children with four or five small-world toys to place on the map.

◼ Encourage the children to play an alternative version of the game 'I spy' by saying the words, 'I spy with my little eye, a toy that is...', then give some positional clues, for example, 'on a grey path', 'beside a house', 'behind a pond' and so on.

◼ Keep giving positional clues until the correct toy has been found, then rearrange the toys to play again.

◼ Help younger children by placing only two toys on the map.

◼ Invite older children to play the game in pairs, one child saying the clues, the other finding the toy.

More ideas

◼ Invite the children to create a map showing a story or rhyme scene, for example, Mary's garden, Red Riding Hood's wood or the Three Little Pigs' town.

◼ Encourage the children to take turns moving a toy character around the scene by following directions given by their partner.

Other curriculum areas

CLL Encourage the children to take turns to describe the position of a character or object within a picture book for the rest of the group to find and identify.

KUW During a local walk, ask the children to describe the position of certain landmarks or points of interest.

Stepping Stone
Find items from positional/directional clues.

Early Learning Goal
Use everyday words to describe position.

◼

Group size
Small groups.

◼

What you need
Green card (approximately 1m x 1m); straight and curved strips of paper in various widths, lengths and colours; shiny paper; glue; small-world toys such as cars, people and animals; small boxes; felt-tipped pens; safe route for a local walk.

Home links
Encourage parents and carers to play traditional 'Hide-and-seek' games with their children that involve clues such as 'Getting hotter!' and 'Getting colder!' to indicate how close or how far the children are from the hidden item.

To the palace

Stepping Stone
Describe a simple journey.

Early Learning Goal
Use everyday words to describe position.

Group size
Small groups.

What you need
A playhouse (or similar); green drapes; strong tape; copy of *The Wizard of Oz* (*Favourite Tales* series, Ladybird Books); PE equipment such as benches, tunnels, hoops, soft mats and large wooden building blocks; area where the children can move freely and safely (indoors or outdoors).

Preparation
Before the children arrive, use the equipment to arrange an obstacle course leading to the playhouse.

What to do
■ Introduce the children to the story *The Wizard of Oz*.
■ Help the children to turn the playhouse into an 'Emerald Palace' using green drapes.
■ Explain that the obstacle course represents the route to the palace.
■ Invite the children to go on an imaginary journey to the 'Emerald Palace' by following the obstacle course.
■ Encourage the children to describe their journey

using terms such as 'along', 'on' and 'under'.
■ Ask the children to think of different ways of using each obstacle, for example, a tunnel could be climbed over, walked around or crawled through.
■ When the children are familiar with the obstacles, encourage them to take turns to describe a journey to the 'palace' for a partner to follow, for example, 'Climb over the tunnel, around the box and along the bench'.
■ Rearrange the obstacles to initiate different journeys and new descriptions.
■ Ask younger children to describe each journey as it occurs, for example, 'I am going over the bench, now I'm going through the tunnel' and so on.
■ Invite older children to help you to rearrange the obstacle course.

More ideas
■ Invite the children to draw an arrow on to several sheets of card and use these as direction markers along the obstacle course.
■ Encourage the children to make a table-top obstacle course for their toys to travel across. Ask them to describe the toys' journey.

Home links
Encourage parents and carers to ask their children to describe where they have been or where they are going while out and about on familiar journeys, asking, for example, 'What do we pass on the way to the shops?'.

Other curriculum areas
KUW Encourage the children to describe simple journeys within your setting, for example, the way to the hall or how to get to the nearest exit.

CLL Ask the children to describe an imaginary journey in a fantasy land such as a treasure island, a strange planet or a giant's castle.

In the woods

What to do
■ Read or tell the children the story of Little Red Riding Hood.
■ Help each child to create two simple puppets of the characters in the story by cutting the photocopiable sheet horizontally in two and gluing the tabs as indicated.

■ Provide interlocking bricks for the children to construct a wall that is big enough for the wolf puppet to hide behind. Then give them brown card to roll and glue into a cylinder to create a hollow log for the wolf to hide in; green card to cut and fold into a bush for the wolf to hide under, and a cardboard tube stuffed at the top with green tissue paper to create a tree for the wolf to hide underneath.
■ Invite the children to use Blu-Tack or masking tape to secure the 3-D models on to a display table to create a woodland scene.
■ Encourage the children to use their puppets for imaginative play about the story and to describe the position of their puppets as they move them around the scene.
■ Help younger children to use positional words, such as 'beside', to describe where a puppet is hiding.
■ Challenge older children to make more detailed descriptions, for example, 'inside the log behind the wall'.

More ideas
■ Read the story 'Goldilocks and the Three Bears' (Traditional), then invite the children to describe the position of three soft-toy bears in the woodland scene.

Other curriculum areas
CLL Encourage the children to talk about the position of the letters in their names, for example, 'J' is the first letter, and 'm' is the last letter in the name 'Jim'.
PD Hold team games and encourage the children to describe the challenges, for example, 'Hop to the hoops by the window, then jump over the ropes on the floor' and so on.

Stepping Stone
Observe and use positional language.

Early Learning Goal
Use everyday words to describe position.
■
Group size
Small groups.
■
What you need
A copy of the photocopiable sheet 'Red Riding Hood' on page 94; interlocking building bricks; cardboard tube; green and brown card; green tissue paper; display table; Blu-Tack or masking tape; a copy of the story 'Little Red Riding Hood' (Traditional).

Home links
Encourage parents and carers to involve their children in making a 3-D scene at home and to use everyday words to describe the position of toys in the scene, for example, animals in a farm set, or characters in a Legoland setting.

Hare and Tortoise

What to do
- Read the story *The Hare and the Tortoise* to the children.
- Invite the children to decorate the programmable toy to represent 'Tortoise'. For example, they could stick on it small squares of brown and orange paper for the pattern of the shell. Draw a face on to a small semicircle of card and attach it to the 'front' of the toy.
- Place the 'Start' and 'Finish' labels on the floor, a reasonable distance apart, to represent the racetrack.
- Encourage younger children to position Tortoise and Hare at the 'Start' sign.
- Tell the children that they are going to play a game by taking it in turns to throw the dice and program Tortoise to move that number of steps towards the 'Finish' sign.
- When Tortoise has moved, invite the children to take turns to move Hare forwards approximately twice the distance.
- When Hare is about half-way between the 'Start' and 'Finish' signs, ask the children to lay him down to have a rest, just as the hare in the story does.
- Invite the children to continue taking turns to throw the dice and to program Tortoise to move forwards.
- When Tortoise reaches the 'Finish' sign, invite a child to pick up Hare and to rush him to the 'Finish' sign. Ask the children who won the race and why.
- Help younger children to program the toy.
- Invite older children to use a dice showing number words, one to six.

More ideas
- Play the game using a long 'racetrack' or a track that has bends.
- Help the children to program Tortoise to move in circles as a dance for joy at winning the race.

Other curriculum areas
PSED   Encourage the children to make up different rules, for example, Hare misses a turn, by resting, every time a 4, 5 or 6 is thrown.

CLL   Help the children to use emergent writing to create instructions for moving Tortoise forwards.

Mathematical development

Teddies' sleepover

What to do
■ Provide the children with the five teddies and the five fabric covers. Let them engage in imaginative play by pretending that the teddies are having a 'sleepover'.
■ Ask the children to put the teddies 'to bed', encouraging them to find out, by trial and error, which cover matches each bear.
■ Next, ask the children to muddle up the covers so that each teddy has a cover that does not fit.
■ Encourage the children to identify which bears have a cover that is too big and which have a cover that is too small.

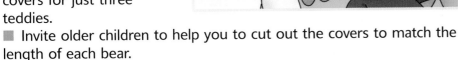

■ Remove the covers and ask the children to place the teddies in order of length.
■ Hold up the longest cover and ask the children to work out which bear it belongs to. Repeat the activity for the other four covers, encouraging language such as 'smallest', 'longest', 'too big' and 'too short'.
■ Encourage younger children to find matching covers for just three teddies.
■ Invite older children to help you to cut out the covers to match the length of each bear.

More ideas
■ Help the children to bend and tape five strips of card to create five simple crowns, one to fit each teddy, for sorting and matching activities.
■ Help the children to each make a simple crown to fit on to their own head. Mix up the crowns and ask the children to find a crown that is too big or too small for them.

Other curriculum areas

PSED Encourage the children to draw and cut out three different-sized bears from brown card. Ask them to attach these to string to create puppets for role-play about the story 'Goldilocks and the Three Bears' (Traditional).
CD Encourage the children to cut fabric into suitable shapes for simple cloaks for teddies to wear.

Shape walk

Stepping Stone
Show awareness of similarities in shapes in the environment.

Early Learning Goal
Use developing mathematical ideas and methods to solve practical problems.

Group size
Small groups.

What you need
A safe outdoor area; A3 copy of the photocopiable sheet 'Shapes around us' on page 95; paper; coloured pencils; display board.

What to do

■ Gather the children together and invite them to look at the enlarged photocopiable sheet. Ask them questions such as, 'Can you find a round window?', 'Can you count the number of square windows?', 'What shape is the door?' and so on.

■ Next, take the children on a walk outside and encourage them to name and identify the shapes of familiar objects, for example,

square paving slabs, oblong bricks and round road signs.

■ Back inside, invite the children to draw one or more of the shaped objects seen during their walk.

■ Talk with the children about the similarities and differences between shapes in the pictures.

■ Mount the children's pictures on to a display board to create a pictorial record of the 'shape walk' and to inspire discussion about the variety of shapes that can be seen in the local environment.

■ Provide younger children with a selection of pre-drawn shapes for them to turn into objects seen during the walk.

■ Invite older children to take with them a clipboard, paper and pencil to draw one or more features when doing the walk outside.

More ideas

■ Provide each child with an A4 copy of the photocopiable sheet. Encourage them to identify objects of the same shape to decorate in a particular colour, for example, round pictures in red and triangular objects in blue.

■ Organise a follow-up walk so that the children can observe shapes in their natural environment.

Other curriculum areas

KUW Help the children to collate a big book showing shapes in nature, for example, leaf and bark rubbings, photographs and samples of flowers, and grasses and leaves to press.

CD Involve the children in creating a collage depicting an imaginary town or garden. Encourage them to design their own flowers, buildings and scenery using a variety of unusual shapes.

Home links
Encourage parents and carers to play observational games with their children by asking them questions while out walking or driving, for example, 'How many triangular signposts can you count on this journey?', 'Can you jump on the round stepping-stones?' and so on.

Colours and patterns

What to do

■ Provide each child with a copy of the photocopiable sheet and three different-coloured pens, pencils or crayons.

■ Help the children to find out how many different colour combinations they can create by colouring each castle on the sheet in a different way, using one or more of their three pens.

■ Talk with the children about the variety of patterns that can be achieved using just three colours. For example, the first castle in one of the columns might have all three sections coloured in red, the second castle might have two sections red, and the third castle just one section red.

■ Ask the children which colours they are using and to explain the 'patterns' or 'sequences' in their own words.

■ Provide younger children with an enlarged copy of the photocopiable sheet and two colours only. Ask them to colour the castles to make them look different. Talk to the children to see if they can tell you why each castle looks different from the next.

■ Invite older children to predict how many different combinations they could make using two or three different colours.

More ideas

■ Play commercial games with the children that involve following or finding a sequence of pictures, colours or patterns, for example, 'Colour Lotto', 'Misfits' and 'Picture dominoes'. Talk with the children about the patterns and arrangements as they play the games.

Other curriculum areas

PSED Provide a group of children with a large outline of a palace drawn on to paper or fabric. Invite them to co-operate as a team to decorate the palace using a repeated pattern of colourful stripes. Add glitter or shiny paper to the stripy palace and display it on the wall to inspire discussion about pattern and colour.

KUW Look at pictures of different homes from around the world. Talk with the children about the variety of shapes, styles and decoration used on the buildings.

Good-night!

What to do
■ Show the children the pictures and examples of different beds and bedding. Talk about the shapes of the beds, blankets, pillows and so on.
■ Invite the children to use the craft materials to each construct a toy bed for one of the dolls.
■ Encourage each child to begin by selecting a box, basket or piece of sponge that is the correct size and shape for their doll to lie on.
■ Then invite them to make sheets, pillows and blankets for the bed by cutting fabric to the correct shape and size.
■ Suggest that the children cut out colourful paper shapes to decorate the headboards, or fabric shapes to decorate the bedding.
■ As the children work, help them to name and identify the 2-D and 3-D shapes, and encourage them to talk about why they have chosen certain shapes for their models.
■ When the toy beds are complete, invite the children to use them with the dolls for imaginative play.
■ Help younger children to make the blankets big enough to cover the doll when placed in the bed.
■ Challenge older children to make a bunk bed or four-poster bed.

More ideas
■ Encourage each child to draw a picture of the bed that they made for their doll.
■ Invite the children to make model wardrobes for their dolls.

Other curriculum areas
CD Encourage the children to begin the activity by sketching a rough plan or design showing the type of bed that they would like to make for their doll.
CLL Ask the children to write or draw about how they made their toy beds or to list the shapes that they used.

Numbers

Name _____

Goals	Assessment	Date
Numbers as labels and for counting		
Say and use number names in order in familiar contexts.		
Count reliably up to 10 everyday objects.		
Recognise numerals 1 to 9.		
Use developing mathematical ideas and methods to solve practical problems.		

Calculating

Name _____

Goals	Assessment	Date
Calculating		
In practical activities and discussion begin to use the vocabulary involved in adding and subtracting.		
Use language such as 'more' or 'less' to compare two numbers.		
Find one more or one less than a number from one to 10.		
Begin to relate addition to combining two groups of objects and subtraction to 'taking away'.		

Photocopiable

Mathematical development

Shape, space and measures

Name _____

Goals	Assessment	Date
Shape, space and measures		
Use language such as 'greater', 'smaller', 'heavier' or 'lighter' to compare quantities.		
Talk about, recognise and re-create simple patterns.		
Use language such as 'circle' or 'bigger' to describe the shape and size of solids and flat shapes.		
Use everyday words to describe position.		
Use developing mathematical ideas and methods to solve practical problems.		

One, two, buckle my shoe

Trace over the lines to write the numbers 1, 3, 5, 7 and 9. Write the numbers 2, 4, 6, 8 and 10 in the empty footprints. Use the rhyme to help you.

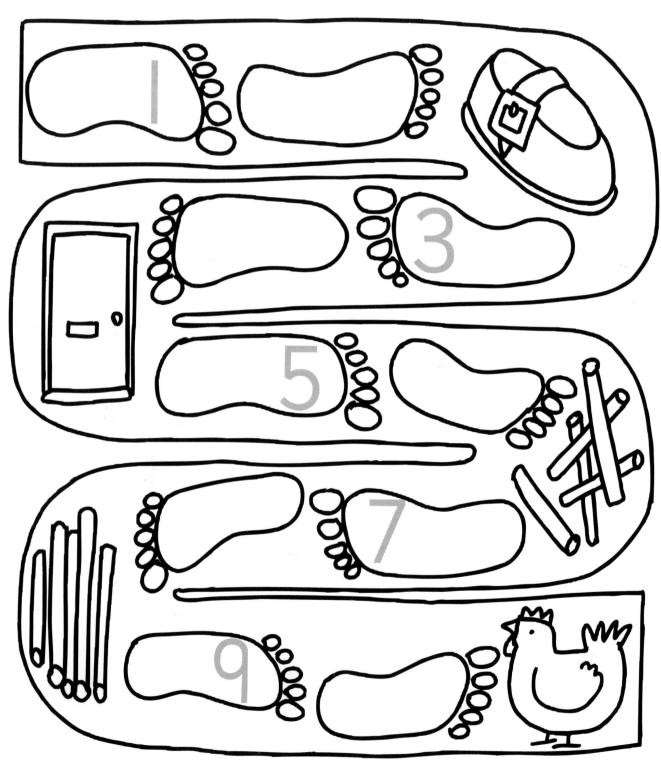

Photocopiable

Mathematical development

Spinner

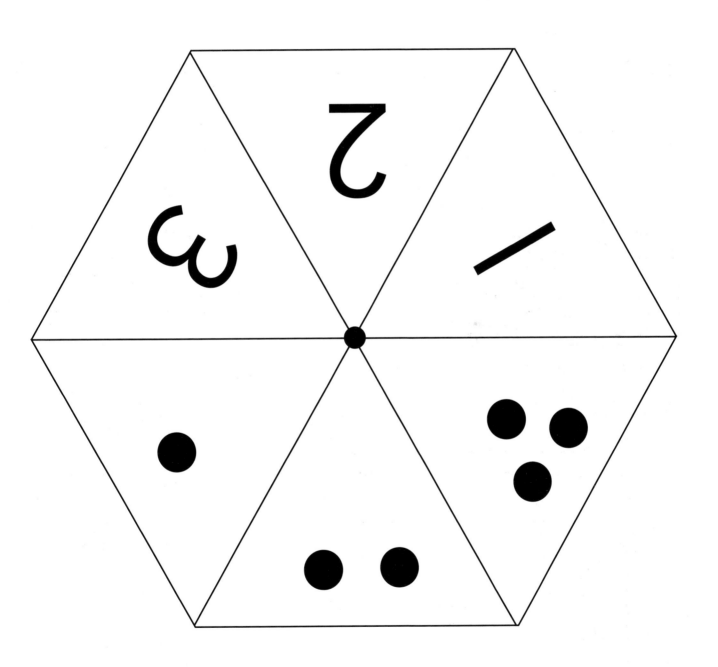

Photocopiable

Crazy creatures

Count how many of each crazy creature are in the picture. How many are there altogether?

How many?

Photocopiable

Mathematical development

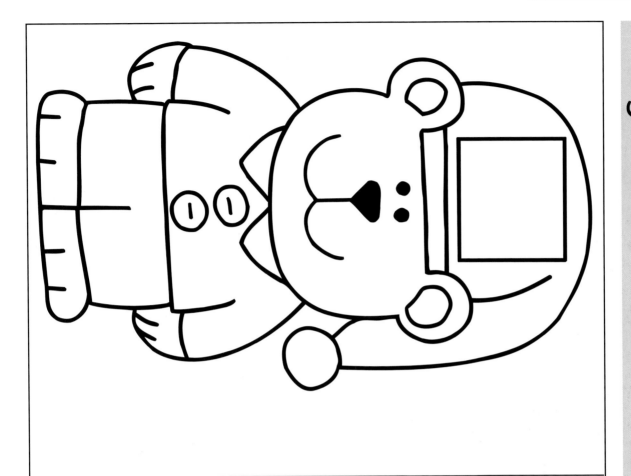

Snug teddies

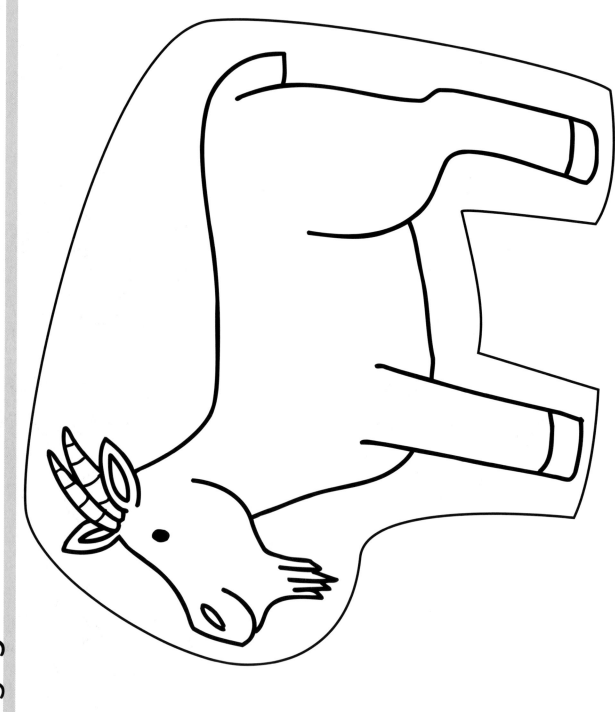

Billy goat

Photocopiable

Mathematical development

Dwarf faces

Colour in and cut out the seven dwarfs' faces. Use them on your models.

Jumping teddy

Photocopiable

Mathematical development

Moving bears

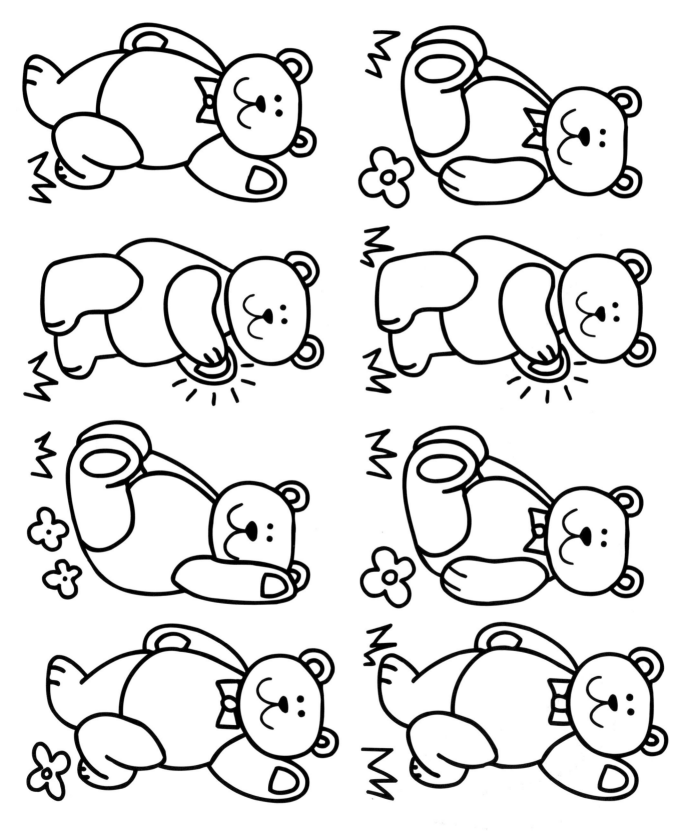

Speckled frog

Photocopiable

Mathematical development

Wiggly worms

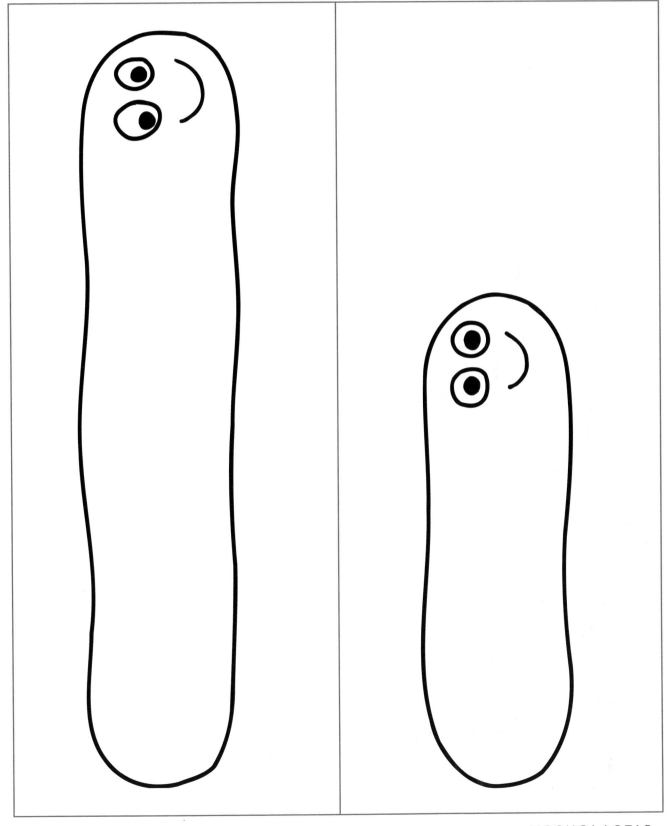

Matching leaves

Photocopiable

Mathematical development

Shapes spiral

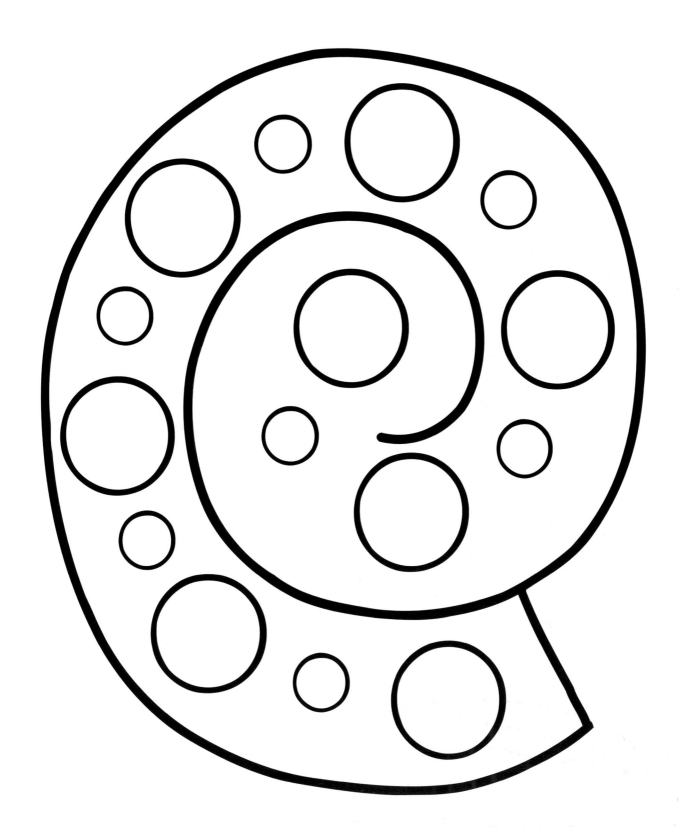

Mathematical development   **Photocopiable**

Red Riding Hood

Red Riding Hood

Back view

glue

glue

glue

glue

Back view

The wolf

Photocopiable

Mathematical development

Shapes around us

Name _____ Date _____

Castles

Name _____   Date _____

Photocopiable   **Mathematical development**